Fixing Capitalism:
Toward A Stable, Efficient Economy

Fixing Capitalism:
Toward A Stable, Efficient Economy

Second Edition

Jonathan A. Carr

ISBN 978-0-578-07702-4

DEDICATED TO

Billie Ruth Carr
1938 – 2010

Love You, Mom.

ACKNOWLEDGEMENTS

Thank you Tamara Black, Marlene Bruce, Christine Ellis, Dr. Kate Hausbeck, James Hendrickson, Dr. Brenda Moore, Dr. George Ritzer, Gail Taylor, and Doug Wagner for all you did for this book. Your feedback, conversation, criticism, and companionship were beyond value, especially in terms of money. Special thanks to the staff and facilities of the Library of Congress in Washington, D.C. where most of this research took place. The Library of Congress was invaluable for a research project such as this that touched on so many disciplines and required many kinds of diverse data. Thank you, thank you, and thank you all.

Table of Contents

Introduction

"Dream no small dreams for they have no
power to move the hearts of men."
--Johann Wolfgang von Goethe

This book is based on research, begun in the early 1990s, which asked the questions: Is it possible to stabilize the economy and make sure there will never be any more economic recessions or depressions? Is it possible to free the economy and everyone in it from the limited supply of money so that the economy works for everyone, no person goes to bed hungry, and we do not have to spend our lives worrying about where we will get ever more and more money? In short, is it possible to make capitalism democratic? Is it possible for every person in every nation to be free to buy whatever they want, without diminishing the quality of life for developed nations? Is economic freedom and economic equality really possible?

As the author pursued these questions during college and graduate school, the project involved researching theories of money in the fields of economics, sociology, economic anthropology and economic history. I broke down the capitalist economy into its four component parts: the open market, supply and demand, the money medium of exchange, and private property, and then analyzed the social effects of each part of capitalism on economic interaction and on the society as a whole. Early in the research, it was clear both that capitalism is already very democratic in many ways, and that the fatal flaw in the capitalist system is the fact that we use a limited commodity, money, to mediate exchange.

The first part of a market economy, an uncorrupted open marketplace, where anyone with a product is free to offer it to the public is a very democratic concept. People who have marketable ideas are free to bring their ideas to the market (if they can find the money to pay for the start-up costs). There is no bureaucrat that they have to bribe to open a store and no politicians using their clout to help their allies by pushing competitors out of the market. The market is open to all comers. They do not even have to be citizens of the country, as is evident by the guys standing outside of moving van rental companies, offering their strong backs to anyone who makes an offer. An uncorrupted open market is a luxury that we take for granted in the United States, but we should not. It is a wonderful thing that we should all be very thankful for.

The rules of supply and demand, the second part of the capitalist economy, where the success or failure of a given product or service depends on businesses competing for and attracting public approval is, again, very democratic. This built-in system, where the needs of the public (or at least the people who have money) drive the evolving economy, makes for a dynamic, fluid, constantly updating economic system.

Even the concept of private property, the third part of the capitalist economy, provides fuel for economic innovation. When consumers see a product and say, "I want that for myself" it forces businesses in the market to provide that product or lose market share to a competitor. The motivation to own something drives the entire economy.

Then there is money: the medium of exchange and the measure of value. It is a limited resource that must be acquired before we can acquire anything else. We all must earn, beg, borrow, or steal some money before we can do anything in the money economy. Money is a unit for measuring value that has its own value separate from what it measures. That is really kind of strange if you think about it. Imagine if a unit of length had value and we fought with each other to acquire little bits of length only to give them away in order to measure something's size or a length of distance? Then we had to go out and do something to acquire more bits of length so that we can measure the length of something else. That would be weird.

It is the global network of money, however, that makes the world economy possible. Every society for thousands of years has created some standardized form of money to make tax collection easier. Modern nations created standard exchange rates with other nations so that their money can be used to trade for goods and services across the globe, enabling trade across the planet.[1] Money is a portable, easily understood, useful measure of value that can be divided to be traded with products of little value or accumulated to be traded with highly valuable products.[2] The global network of money is the web that carries the global network of production, distribution, and consumption.

---

[1] Ingham, 2001, p. 313, Maurer, 2006, p. 18.
[2] Jevons, 1875, p. 31.

It is also the limitations of the money commodity that most divide us and holds the economy back from producing everything that we need and that the environment could sustainably provide. The most obvious limitation of the money commodity is the fact that no person, organization, business or government has enough of it. Research shows that even people who have money report on average that they would be happy if they could have just twenty percent more.[3] When they get twenty percent more, inflation has eroded the value of that money and their desires have expanded, so they estimate they will need just twenty percent more. Just twenty percent more, then twenty percent more, and twenty percent more in an endless cycle.

Money is a scarce resource and that scarcity is central to our relationship with money. That scarcity is the fatal flaw in the money economy and in the economy as a whole. The limited supply of money as was mentioned above limits the amount of resources that our producers can take from the environment, because they only take what our money supply allows us to buy, which is much less than the environment could support. Here is a diagram to illustrate:

Supply and Demand Filtered Through the Money Supply

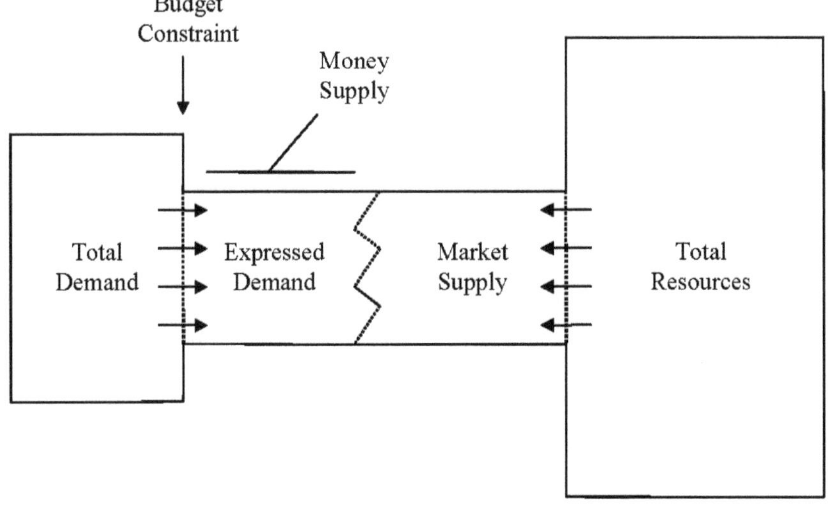

[3] Easterlin, 2002.

As the above diagram shows, the total amount of human wants and needs, the total demand, can only be expressed if money exists to pay for that demand.[4] That expressed demand goes into the marketplace and insists that someone fulfill its needs. The suppliers take the resources from the environment to meet that need, create the product, and sell it to the consumer.[5] That is how money capitalism works and that is why it can never keep up with the thousands of new goods and services, or the tens of millions of consumers, that enter the market every year. The supply of money just cannot keep up, especially when we factor in inflation, which diminishes the power of money, and greed, which concentrates the money supply in the hands of people who already have the most of it.

The scarcity of money not only limits what we have; it also limits what we can do, where we can go, what we can learn, and what dreams we can realize. That is the real tragedy of the money economy. Imagine the brilliant children who have the potential to find the answers to the great problems of their day, find cures for diseases, negotiate the impossible peace agreements, invent that product that will make our lives so much better, or just become those everyday heroes: doctors, teachers, firemen, if only they had not been born to poor parents in a refugee camp in a war torn province of an impoverished nation. That is an extreme example of course.

Even poor kids in wealthy nations have their potential limited by their limited money and that is not just a tragedy for them; it is a tragedy for the whole world. That poor kid who cannot afford college might have become the one teacher who could really inspire one of our children to be their best. The existence or absence of money determines far too much outside the realm of economic exchange. The limited supply of money holds most people back from doing everything they could do with their lives, and it holds the economy back from producing all of the goods and services that people would buy if only they had the money.

That scarcity also creates the boom and bust business cycle because of the volatile changes in the volume of money flowing through the economy as we all decide how much money we are going

---

[4] Adam Smith, 1776, pp. 158-9.

[5] "All supply converges on money, and all demand emanates from money" Helferrich, 1927, p. 280.

to spend or not spend. When we consumers as a group feel confident about the amount of money we will have in the future, we spend more, which leads to more production, employment, and consumption. A lack of confidence leads to less spending, less production, and higher unemployment. As the mass psychology of consumer confidence wavers back and forth between *spend* and *don't spend*, the health of the entire economy is jostled back and forth from boom to bust.

Finally any scarce, powerful commodity will illicit greed among us human beings. Greed for this valuable medium reverberates throughout our world contributing to social division, hatred, and even war. So here we know that the money medium of exchange is both the solution for making the economy work and the central problem with the economy. What do we do when the key to the global economy is also the fatal flaw in the global economy? That was a puzzle.

And then the internet was born: a global information network where the medium, information, has no inherent value because information is infinite and giving it away does not exhaust one's supply. It was clear early in the research that the internet has the potential to make the global economy work, without becoming an obstacle for making the economy work for everyone. To fix capitalism, we have to replace the limited network of money with the infinite information network. Money after all does little more than represent the value of goods, services and labor, and then communicate that value to the world. Value is just a number and the internet is very good at communicating numbers around the world. The internet can do that job very well.

Once we replace the limited economic medium, money, with the unlimited economic medium, information, we can have a direct relationship with the environment and use all of its resources to provide for every person on the planet. Supply and demand will look like this:

Supply and Demand in a Networked Economy

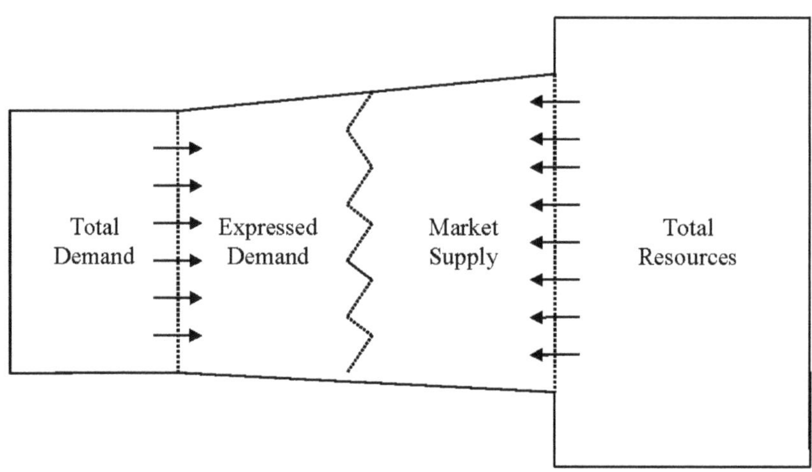

To take advantage of the internet's potential, the research examined the role that money plays in our lives and our society, and replicated that role using technology. I created a system for businesses to compete for consumer patronage in an open market, according to the rules of supply and demand, without using money to mediate exchange. I created a measure of productivity to ensure that the economy remains lean and efficient. I earned master's degree in economic sociology while I created this new system for organizing our economic lives. It has been ten years since I finished this project, this non-monetary accounting system, and now might be the right time for it.

What will networked capitalism look like? How will we structure the rules of competition? How will we ensure high productivity and dynamic innovation? How will we handle unemployment? People have to eat even if they are not working, and we need them to quickly find more work and provide us all with the fruits of their labor. How will we transition from the money economy to the networked economy? What will society look like afterwards? What will we lose? What industries will be eliminated in a moneyless economy? How many of the government functions will be eliminated when we do not need them to regulate the financial sector and offset the inequalities of a money economy with welfare programs? Read on and see.

Chapter 1

What Needs to Be Fixed?

Something is very wrong with the modern capitalist economy, and we now have the technology to fix it.

The global market economy is not doing its job in even the most fundamental sense: providing the world with the most basic human needs. One fifth of humanity, 1.4 billion people, lives in poverty and 1.2 billion people go without access to clean drinking water.[6] Twenty-five thousand (25,000) people die of hunger every day[7] while the global economy produces more food than people need and is capable of producing much more. Only thirty percent of humanity lives in fully developed economies, which means that seventy percent of the global economy could be doing more for all of us.[8] Meanwhile, every year the world economy gains 76 million mouths to feed, clothe, house, educate and employ.[9] Even in 'developed' economies when the economy is growing and unemployment is low, one in eight people and one in six children still live in poverty.[10] Our needs are clearly not being met by our economy.

Even those of us with plenty of resources suffer from the weaknesses in the market economy. Persistent volatility in the market, with growth bubbles and painful recessions, buffet our finances and our lives, making the economy very difficult to manage even in the most developed economies. One downturn in the market can wipe out our savings, destroy the value in our homes, destroy our dreams, undermine the lives we want for our children, yank us out of

---

[6] World Bank Poverty Analysis: http://go.worldbank.org/K7LWQUT9L0 and the 2006 United Nations Human Development Report: http://hdr.undp.org/en/reports/global/hdr2006/

[7] UNICEF: http://www.childinfo.org/mortality.html

[8] United Nations Human Development Index: http://hdr.undp.org/en/statistics/

[9] U.S. Census Bureau: http://www.census.gov/cgi-bin/ipc/pcwe

[10] U.S. Census Bureau: http://www.census.gov/prod/2009pubs/p60-236.pdf

retirement, and reveal the truth about all of those promises the financial people told us.

This volatility also makes it nearly impossible to export capitalism to 'developing' nations around the world where they may also be held back by fewer natural resources, political corruption, extreme levels of poverty, recent warfare, and a less educated, less productive workforce.

So, what can we do to make the economy work? The old rule of thumb in government is that we can tell a public system is working when nobody notices it. The sewer system is a good example. Who thinks about the tunnels under the street that take away our waste? We think about it when the sewers run over into our daily lives. The sewers have to come to us, before we give them a moment's thought. The same rule goes for the water treatment systems, the meat inspection system, public transportation, the electric grid, the highway system, and the system we use to count votes on Election Day.

What if we could make the economy work so smoothly, so stable and efficient, that we never again give the economy a second thought? What if we had an economy that automatically did its job, where businesses compete to create and distribute goods and services throughout the world in amounts that meet every person's needs, and we all spend our time living our lives, tending to our families, and dreaming our dreams? We now have the technology to create that economy.

Imagine an economy that works like a well-functioning electric grid. The grid is a network out there doing its job, generating and distributing electricity throughout the country. When we need electricity, we go to the wall and flip a switch or plug in a machine, and there is electricity. We always just assume the electricity will be there. If we buy more electronic things and need more electricity, we expect the grid to increase its capacity to generate more electricity to meet our increased demand.[11]

---

[11] Of course this is an imperfect metaphor because there are times that the electric grid fails us. We have black outs and brown outs at times and the government asks us to use less electricity to lower demand on the electric grid. However, this is the effect of the limited money supply on the electric grid, preventing governments from upgrading their infrastructure when tax dollars are needed for other more immediate goals. A networked economy will relieve us all from the budget constraint and enable power companies to upgrade their services just like every other industry in the networked economy.

Imagine there is an economic network out there that automatically creates the goods and services that we demand of it without any payment, limited only by the bounds of nature. When we need food, clothes, medical care, a vacation or what ever, we will go to a store, hospital, travel agent, or where ever and there they will be. What if the economic network automatically adjusted its level of production for different goods and services to the total societal level of demand, because that was its job? Businesses will automatically adjust to serve our demand as it ebbs and flows without any budget restrictions. We will just assume that goods and services will be there for us the same way we assume that electricity will be there for us. Some day that is exactly what the economy will be: a big network, designed to create and distribute whatever we demand from it.

This improvement will stabilize the economy so there are no more recessions or depressions. Stability will make the economy much easier to manage, and it will make launching an affluent economy in a 'developing' nation as easy as installing the hardware, training the population, and saying 'Go'. Finally, stability will make the economy more resilient against sudden shocks like natural disasters, global warming, terrorist attacks or whatever else our future holds.

This change will also enable the economy to produce enough goods and services to meet the needs of every person in the world, all while maintaining an environment of vibrant, dynamic competition between businesses. We can create a stable capitalist economy, where everyone in the world can get what they need freely in an open market, according to the rules of supply and demand, thanks to our new global information network: the internet.

Consider this question: Why do we each need money on a daily basis? We need money because when we go to the store, if we want to buy something, the store wants money in return for what we want. Why do the stores need money? They need money because they need to buy goods and services from distributors, the electric company, their employees, etc. and *they* all want money. The maker of each product needs money to get the raw materials from the farmer, the lumber company, the steel producer, or whomever takes the raw materials from nature, who also want money in return for their product. We do not pay Mother Nature for her resources of course.

That is the role of money in the economy from the point of view of the buyer. Another way to think of the economy's relationship to money is from the perspective of the seller. Businesses only buy enough inventory from their suppliers that they know they can sell to consumers. Inventory suppliers and utility companies like water and electric companies only create as much inventory, water and electricity as they know they can sell to businesses and consumers. The fisheries, farmers, lumber and mining companies only take as much from nature as they know they can sell to businesses to sell to consumers. In other words, the economy does not use the full resources of nature in making our goods and services. The economy only harvests the limited amount that the limited supply of money allows people to purchase.

There is a chain of traded goods and services between the consumer and nature, and every step of the chain requires money to make that purchase, that step in the chain, happen. That is how we organize our economy. In short, we all need money because for thousands of years, we have used money to organize our economy. Money has been a part of our lives, our dreams, our successes, our failures, and even our deaths for so long that we cannot imagine life without it. The reality is, though, if we found another way to organize the economy without using money, we would not need money.

For example, what if all of those people in the chain between the consumer and nature had an agreement? What if they were members of a special network, where just for the members of that network, everyone agreed to do their jobs without payment? Think about a small town where the grocers, the farmers, the carpenters, the plumbers, the auto mechanics, the utilities, every business agreed to give each other what they needed without payment. If everyone in the town got what they needed without payment, no person would need money.

Businesses today make these agreements all the time, on small scales. Businesses that know each other do favors for each other and the owners just give each other a wink of the eye. The plumber helps the barber with his pipes and the barber gives the plumber free haircuts. The pizza store owner provides the pies for the weekly card game, where the grocery store owner has brought the drinks and the baker has brought the desserts. The baker's smart aleck brother comes to the game and just mooches off everyone else, but he is a good guy and he provides some comic relief, so nobody complains.

When the author was a teenager, he worked in a Mexican food restaurant that was owned by a guy who also owned a pizza place. Anyone who has worked in a restaurant knows that when we work in restaurants we get tired of eating our own food all the time. So, every now and then one of the stores' managers would call the other and say, "Want to trade?" And of course they did. The pizza place would deliver pizza and pick up Mexican food to take back to the people working at the pizza place. As a rule, the owner provided free food to both sets of employees, so he did not care.

What if all of those people in the global economic chain between the consumer and nature got their food, their electricity, and their families were clothed, housed, educated, etc. with everyone doing their jobs for free? If everyone had an agreement to give everyone else what they needed, without payment, we would not need money. If the members of this network only had to show their membership identification to each other, and in return they could take what they needed from the store, they would not need money and they could get whatever they needed. The internet can make that kind of agreement possible. We can turn the economy into a big economic network and then we can have that kind of agreement among the whole global economy. And then nobody would need money. Policy makers in turn could focus on using all of the earth's resources to sustainably meet every person's needs instead of focusing on managing our limited money supply and improving consumer confidence.

The next generation of capitalism, networked capitalism, will be an open access economic network where private property will be traded in an open market, according to the laws of supply and demand, just like in a modern capitalist economy. The upgrade will be that the economy will use the internet to coordinate global exchange, instead of using a network of money to mediate exchange. We will create nonmonetary rules for businesses to compete under and we will use the internet to measure value, keep track of supply and demand, and determine which businesses succeed or fail.

The All-You-Can-Eat Economy

The limited supply of money, as was mentioned, limits the amount of goods and services that the economy can produce because producers will only take as much from the environment as our budgets allow us to buy. As long as we use a limited medium like money, we can not fully use the environment to meet the needs of the entire population. Because of the realities of money, we are not really interacting with the environment; we are interacting with the money supply. Information, unlike money, is infinite and a networked economy will enable the economy to produce as many goods and services as the environment can sustain. In short, businesses will be able to increase production dramatically to better meet everyone's needs.

We will all be able to acquire whatever we want from the economy without worrying about money. How? We will change the rules of the economy. To use a restaurant metaphor, right now we have a sort of "a la carte" economy where we make money and then buy something, then make more money and buy something else. We also have to save some money today so that we can buy things later when we are not making money any more.

In the networked economy, we will have more of an all-you-can-eat economic model where people will pay one entry price, contributing to the economic network by doing jobs we love, and in return we will have full access to the economic network, taking whatever we need in terms of goods and services. Later in the book I compare the new rules to citizenship, where a citizen of a democratic nation has full access to the political system and all of the rights and privileges that go along with citizenship. A person in a networked economy will have a right to the full benefits of the advanced economy by virtue of their economic citizenship. Citizenship will be established by working for an accredited business in the networked economy.

Businesses will increase their production and compete with each other to keep up with the increased demand when people can acquire anything they desire. The first thing we will do is create nonmonetary rules for competition based on the number of products businesses sell and the number of customers they serve, instead of competing based on the amount of money they make. We will compare businesses' sales to their competitors and require all of them to maintain a certain minimum market share in order for businesses to keep their licenses and have access to the economic network.

Like individuals, a business that proves its value to the economy by maintaining a minimum market share will have full access to the wholesalers, distributors and everyone else they need in the network to supply and staff their business. A business that fails to attract customers will lose their access to the network and be forced to close. This is how we will keep the economy lean, competitive and adaptive to the needs of the population. Give people what they want and keep the business license, lose too much of consumers' interest and thank you, but please close your shop.

As businesses innovate, advertise, and update their offerings to attract customers away from their competitors, they will maintain a vibrant, competitive economy. It is worth emphasizing that when we take money out of the economy and coordinate free exchange with the internet, businesses will also have unlimited resources to advertise and innovate in order to improve their services, attract customers and increase their market share. That will lead to an even more competitive market than we have now. Smaller businesses will come up with new innovations to attract customers and secure their market share, forcing larger businesses to innovate to keep up.

Common Questions and Comments

Before we get started talking about how we can improve the economy, we have to get four questions out of the way that always come up when I discuss networked capitalism. I also need to introduce a feature of this book: The “Common Comment”. This idea, networked capitalism, always generates numerous questions. Therefore, as the text progresses, I will introduce questions that often pop up and then I will answer them. For example:

Common Comment: Is this communism?

This is capitalism. This is about open, decentralized markets and vibrant, creative competition between businesses. The cold war is over and capitalism won! Communism is dead as a theory for managing large economies. Even the old communist nations are not so communist anymore. This is a new idea, not communism or traditional capitalism. It is the next step in the evolution of capitalism, where private property is still traded in an open market, according to the rules of supply and demand. The difference is that the exchange will be networked and coordinated with the internet instead of mediated with money. This will stabilize the economy, prevent recessions and depressions, and enable the economy to increase production dramatically to efficiently meet everyone’s needs.

I love making money just as much as the next guy. I used to be a wealth manager after all. Please don’t hate me for it. I never promised my clients more than I could deliver. However, in spite of loving money, I know that we can manage our economy better. I am a little like the Ferrari driver who knows that a fuel-efficient Tesla will also stimulate the senses, without spewing pollution in the air. The money economy works just fine for me and maybe twenty percent of humanity. While it is working for some of us, though, it is doing damage to many other people and places. Plus, now I know that there is a better way for me and everyone else to get all of those great things out of the economy. This will bring affluence to the world, make us all safer, and be better for everyone in the long run.

My job when I worked in investments was to make other people wealthy. If we do this right, we can make everyone wealthy! Everyone around the world can feel the real wealth of a comfortable, healthy lifestyle where they can dream their dreams, work to realize those dreams, raise their families, and then retire in peace. Networked capitalism will be a decentralized market economy, not communism.

Communism, just to really address the question, is a centrally controlled economy[12] where the government bureaucracy decides what goods are made and how much variety people have. As I said above, networked capitalism will be a decentralized market economy. The internet will coordinate exchange, and everyday people like you and me will control the economy with our decisions about which products we like and do not like, just like we do in a capitalist money economy. The role of government will actually decrease when they will no longer control how much we can buy through changes in the interest rates or the tax rates.

The government also will no longer be in the business of redistributing wealth, so all of those departments that exist to take money from tax payers and give services to the poor will be closed. Do you like the idea of smaller government? The government will be a lot smaller and less intrusive in a networked capitalist economy.

Common Comment: Then it is socialism, that's for sure!

It is not socialism either. Socialism is government ownership of land and property for the public good. All of the goods and services in the networked economy, including real estate, will be privately owned.

---

[12] See Milton Friedman, 1962, p. 13: "Fundamentally, there are only two ways of coordinating the economic activities of millions. One is central direction involving the use of coercion—the technique of the Army and of the modern totalitarian state. The other is voluntary cooperation of individuals—the technique of the market place." Networked Capitalism will be a market economy that coordinates the voluntary cooperation of free individuals.

Of course there will still be public land and property like parks, highways, sewer systems and the like, which are used for the public good and are therefore technically socialistic. However, networked capitalism is an economic system where private property is traded in an open market according to the rules of supply and demand, with minimal government interference.

More importantly, though, this book is not about ideology; it is about technology. My conservative friends like that we are going to shrink the government and make the capitalist economy stable. Nobody likes the government interfering in our lives, and when they no longer feel the need to counter the inequalities of money capitalism, the government will have to close all of those bureaucracies, and they will have less of a role in our lives. We could shrink the United States government down to the size it was before World War II and all of the government programs of the welfare state.

Conservatives also do not like the wild boom-and-crash fluctuations that a money economy goes through. Recessions cost us money and are dangerous to all our well-being. Even those who invest only in bonds did not like it that some bond markets froze up during the Great Recession and they could not sell their bonds when they wanted to sell. The networked economy will be a system of production and distribution that we never have to worry about. We will be able to live our lives in financial peace and equality, just like many of us now live in political peace and equality.

My progressive friends like it that the economy will benefit everyone. They like reading the Declaration of Independence and seeing it written there that we are all created equal. They like the idea that everyone should be free and equally able to pursue their life, liberty and happiness as they see fit, and they know everyone's lack of money gets in the way of those supposedly inalienable rights. Moving to a networked economy is the key to making that a reality for everyone around the world.

Both groups like it that the crime rate will go down. Crime will not pay in a networked economy because we will have the power to decide who has access to the economic network. In networked capitalism, economic power will come from either owning an accredited business, or working for one. There will no longer be a medium of exchange that bad people can use for bad purposes. Drug cartels will have nothing economically to gain from distributing addiction. All of the money related crimes like bribery, fraud, embezzlement, prostitution, counterfeiting, etc. will go extinct when we get rid of money.

We will finally be able to put aside the nonstop fighting over money, taxes, and spending in our political debates, and really develop as a society. Remember back in the mid-twentieth century when technology was going to solve all of our problems? We were all going to fly around with jetpacks, nuclear energy would be too cheap to meter, there would be no poverty, and everyone would have robot butlers? Well, in 2009 an engineer from New Zealand introduced what may be the first commercially viable jetpack. This year I am introducing a way to get rid of poverty and help every kid afford a robot butler. So, we are getting there!

This new adaptation to the capitalist economy is just that, a technological adaptation. It is not a conservative adaptation or a progressive adaptation. It will not prove one side right and the other side wrong. The economy is just a tool. The economy can be used for conservative ends or progressive ends. It is just an economy. It will more efficiently take the resources of the environment and use them to meet our needs. Networking capitalism will solve a lot of problems, but do not worry; we will have plenty more problems left behind.

Common Comment: Who will control this networked economy?

The economy will be controlled by the same people who control the internet: nobody. A good economy functions on its own, without anybody trying to wrestle it down and force it to fulfill one goal or another. Networked capitalism will be a good economy. The internet will be used to coordinate exchange, measure supply and demand, and keep track of the competitive economy. It will be how we express our economic desires, just like we now hand over money to express demand for a good or service. Once we develop rules for the competition between businesses, the economy will function on its own without government interference or control by special interests, which is the way it should be. State and local governments will be in charge of compiling and publishing the sales data that will be used to measure competition and determine which businesses succeed or fail, but that will be more of an accounting role.

With those questions answered, on to Chapter 2 which will discuss how each of us will live and thrive in the networked economy.

Chapter 2

Democracy, the Economy and Employment

Employment and the Networked Economy

How will we all fit into a networked economy? The reader may have noticed from the introduction that I compared networked capitalism to democracy. In a democracy the rule is that if we are citizens of the country, we are free to vote, run for office, and compete with our fellow citizens to become the most powerful person in the country if we want to. Democracy also does away with the extremes of political power: no more dictator, no more slave. In a democracy, we have records of who is a citizen. If we want to vote or run for office, we must first prove our citizenship with these records, and then we are free to vote or to run for office.

When I started thinking about competing without money, I used democracy as my template. Who is a "citizen" of the economy? A citizen of a democracy is a person who lives there and has proven that they have a stake in the nation's well-being, either by birth or by residence followed by taking a citizenship test. It seems logical, then, that a "citizen" of the economy is a person or a business that has a stake in the economy. If a person is gainfully employed and the economy is supporting their lifestyle, they certainly have a stake in its well-being. If a business is actively involved in the production and distribution of goods and services, and the economy supports their well-being, then it has a stake in the well-being of the economy.

Following this simple logic, I propose that we create an economy in which economic citizenship, i.e. employment, enables full, equal access to the economic network. This will be the same as how citizenship provides individuals with equal access to the political system. An employed person will be able to acquire whatever they need from any store, any vendor, any medical provider, and any restaurant in the global economy, without limit.

Common comment:	***Wait a minute! You mean that if I have a job, I can walk into any store and walk out with whatever I want?***

You will have to go through the checkout line so the store can keep track of what you are taking and replenish their inventory, but that is right. Whatever you want, you can take. As a person who contributes to the economic network, you will have a right to full access to all of the goods and services available inside of the network. That will be the right of every person who contributes to the economy, as well as their dependents.

Common comment:	***That makes no sense. If people can take whatever they want, they will walk out with the whole store, and then the owner won't have a store!***

Why would they do that? Think about that for a moment. What could they do with all of those products? Say they drove a big eighteen-wheeled truck to the front door of a grocery store, opened up the back of the truck, went into the store, and started carrying out the whole inventory, loading it into the back of the truck. So when they are finished, they have a big truck full of all kinds of fruits and vegetables, canned goods, pasta, soups, fresh meats, milk and dairy products, boxed cereals, books and magazines, all kinds of candy and snack foods, that overpriced hardware equipment that some stores sell, cleaning products, etc. These people drive away with all of these things in the back of the big truck. What will they do with it?

Common comment:	***They will sell it! Won't they?***

To whom? Think about it. They pull the truck down the street or even drive across the country. They park on the side of the road and flip open the back of the truck. Are they going to stand their at the back of the truck with a megaphone and start calling to the crowd? "Get your fresh beef here! We have some wonderful meat here, folks.

Step right up to my refrigerated truck and buy all of the groceries you need."

Remember, *everybody* can go into any store and get whatever they want. The whole global economy is one big network where every person has full access to the network. They can have what ever they want out of real, air-conditioned stores that they have been going to for years, with clean floors and plenty of room to browse the shelves for whatever products they might need. If you could walk into any grocery store and get as much food as you wanted, would you get food from some creepy guy with food in the back of his truck?

Common comment:	***OK, they won't sell it. But they will fill up their houses. What about electronics? People will get a hundred flat-screen televisions for their houses.***

The chapter on living in a networked economy discusses what will happen to greed when everyone can own anything. We return to the restaurant metaphor and the all-you-can-eat establishment. Does a person pile up several plates at the all-you-can-eat buffet, eat a little, and then throw the rest out? No. When people can have whatever they want, they take what they need and then leave the rest.

There might be some people who would go crazy with the gadgets, but most people would not. Think about it this way. If we network the global economy and enable every person to buy whatever they need freely, we are basically making everyone like billionaires. They can buy whatever they want. Does a billionaire have piles and piles of electronics in their homes? Have you seen those television shows that take the viewers for a tour through wealthy people's homes? The homes are not piled to the rafters with television sets. They are elegantly decorated with fine furnishings. The wealthy people on these shows have some supercharged toys and some have vast collections of expensive things like classic cars, art, or old jewels, like Faberge eggs. When you think about it, though, people will not fill their homes with gadgets?

It does seem logical, however, that for some people who have nothing, who suddenly can have anything, there will be a few who go crazy. We will see many interesting reactions to this new economy from the first generation of people who live through the transition. As the global economy works itself into a pattern, however, people will get used to the idea that the global economic network is there to provide us with whatever goods and services we want. Those few people who went crazy will look around and wonder what all of that clutter is for. Succeeding generations, who will grow up with the new economy as the accepted reality will not buy wastefully like that.

Other people might buy more than they need, to stock up, because they will not be sure the new economy is going to work out. This is called hoarding. People hoard things when they are afraid and think there will be shortages in the future. If they trust that what they will need tomorrow will be there when they go to the store tomorrow, they will not hoard things today. As a society we will need to increase production to satisfy many more of everyone's needs. Using more recyclable materials and then recycling products after we use them will be much more important, to meet the increased demand. And if we do it right, we will be able to satisfy enough needs so that people will have confidence in the system and will not panic.

As we will also see later, the transition process from a money economy to a networked economy will be very slow, so that people understand what is happening and trust that everything is going to work just fine. When people understand what is going on and what will come next, they will not panic and hoard things. They will buy what they need and enjoy their lives.

Sustainability and Overconsumption

Common comment: ***This still won't work, because if everyone consumed like some people do, we will use up all of our resources!***

It can work. But you are right: we will finally have to face the problem of providing for every human being on the planet. In the past, the limited supply of money was an easy scapegoat for not creating viable economies in developing nations and for not feeding the world. We could all sit back and say that we would love to help, but we just don't have the money to feed everyone. People did not expect the economy to meet everyone's needs. We expected the money economy to leave a certain percentage of people out of luck, and that is exactly what it has done.

When we network the economy, however, our producers will be able to take as many resources from the environment as they need to meet public demand. Farmers, miners, fisheries, lumber companies, etc., will be able to use all of the resources of nature to sustainably provide for our needs. We will have the capacity, and the expectation, for the economy to use every available resource to meet the needs of the entire global population.

Plus, it is important to remember that relatively few people in the world really want to consume like "some people" do. Some cultures actually find it obscene to consume that much, to fill one's life with that many things, and to get too fat. However, even for people who do like to consume, the economy does not have to provide every product that every person wants. People understand that they cannot have everything they want. People will not take to the streets if they do not have the latest version of the latest gadget, so that they have to make do with the last version of that gadget. The networked economy will have to produce more goods and services than the money economy does now, which it certainly will, and enough goods and services so that people will accept the system. Frankly, if they have accepted the money system, with the terrible job that it does providing for people, any improvement will be heartily welcomed.

Food, water and housing will be the most important, must-do, drop-dead-if-we-don't things to provide, though, and this is completely possible to accomplish if we would only try. We have the capacity to produce enough food and water to satisfy the world, which is why it is so important to develop water resources. We also have enough materials on this rocky planet to build all the homes we want, so we will be able to build homes for all of those displaced people once we do not have to worry about finding the money to pay the homebuilders.

Outside of the resources of nature, we can also develop more recyclable synthetic materials that we can use in manufacturing, which will enable us to manufacture many more products and then recycle the synthetic material, to be used in the next generation of products. As we develop more materials that we can reuse over and over again, we can rely less and less on the bounty of nature. In a networked economy, the research industry will also be relieved of a budget constraint, which will lead to many innovations that we have yet to even dream of, to produce goods and services for the population.

Governments around the developing world, and in the developed world, will also have the economic power to build their infrastructures to make their part of the global network more efficient. They can build better roads, sanitation systems, electric grids, and water processing systems. They can desalinate ocean water, if needed, to irrigate arid land and provide potable water to their population. They can also improve their education system to better train their population. All of these improvements will increase the productive capacity of the global economy and enable us all to provide for many more people than we are serving today.

The other good news, as I have mentioned, is that 70 percent of our global economy is currently underdeveloped, and could produce many more goods and services. Think of all of those people who are living in squalor and could be using their labor to contribute to the global economy. Think of all of the unexplored and unsurveyed portions of the globe that have untapped resources. For example, the American forces in Afghanistan discovered vast mineral resources in the mountains of Afghanistan worth many times the nation's Gross National Product. The Afghan economy, however, is not properly organized to take the minerals from the ground. We have no idea how much can really be taken from the global environment to provide goods and services to the global economy.

If we can put a person on the moon, however, we can find a way to feed every human being. Once they are free of the budget constraint, the nations of the world will increase food production by every means, including reclaiming desert lands, irrigating every place that food can be grown, and stopping the use of food for automobile fuel.

We can also begin using alternative methods that are too expensive in a money economy. Certain foods can be grown in vertical growing systems being developed that do not need fertile land at all. The food is grown suspended in vertical plastic sheets with rows and columns of pockets where the seeds are planted and nourished with sprayed water and nutrients. Small garden foods like lettuce, broccoli, tomatoes, cabbages, etc. can be grown in this way. This growing method does not require fertile land and actually grows food at a much higher density per square area of land than traditional growing in the earth.

If these foods were no longer planted in the ground, we could allocate farmland for plants that actually require vast tracks of land like grains. In the meantime, these vertical farms could be created in areas that are otherwise useless. Necessity is the mother of invention and this will be a necessity. The power of human innovation will lead us to meet the needs of our friends and neighbors.

Sustainable development will also become absolutely vital to our survival. We have many people on this planet and this new economy will give us the ability to consume this planet dry if we are not careful. Maintaining balancing in the amount of resources that we take from the environment is a more natural challenge than the ones we face in a money economy. In a money economy, professionals face problems like "How can we create a better sales technique so that consumers do not realize that this new type of mortgage product is not a good idea?"

Again, recycling will become much more important. We might reopen mines that are not viable in a money economy but still contain valuable metals. We can mine old garbage dumps and junk yards for metal, rubber and anything else useful. That may seem like a strange idea, but when the economy is free of the budget constraint, it will reach out wherever there are resources to meet the needs of the population.

Here is another strange idea, there is also an asteroid belt out there in space with trillions of tons of heavy metals that could be brought back to earth and used. There is one "Near Earth" asteroid floating not too far away, 20 million miles, called "Asteroid 1986 DA" that is 1.2 miles wide and contains 10,000 tons of gold, 100,000 tons of platinum, 10 billion tons of iron, and a billion tons of nickel.[13] Without the budget constraint of a money economy, our only limit will be our limitless imagination. We will imagine great ways to meet the needs of the whole population.

Social Issues Caused by Unlimited Consumption

Common comment:	***People will fight you because they want their money to make them look like they are better than other people. If anyone can buy anything, then a janitor can buy a mansion. People won't like that.***

You know, you are right about that one. In a money economy we measure everything with money including our own self worth and the societal worth of everyone around us. Many people see the drive for more and more money as a test of their own self worth and when they get to a place in life where they have plenty of money, they feel like

[13] "Gems in Space – Undreamed Treasures in a Passing Nugget" *The Seattle Times*, June 8, 1991.

they have won the game of capitalism. Of course if they won the game, it means that other people have lost the game and the 'winners' can feel good about themselves and their victory. In that sense we do use money to make us feel like we are better than other people.

We also kid ourselves that the lucrative job that makes more money is more valuable to society than the job that makes less money in our economy. That of course is a silly notion. Every job provides an invaluable contribution to the overall economy. For example, imagine if every bank president in the world took this summer off from work. Imagine they all went to some island in the Mediterranean and sipped frosty drinks for a few months this year.

In Europe that happens every August. Practically the whole continent takes off the month of August. If all of the Chief Executive Officers took the summer off, the world would certainly keep spinning. There would be a shortage of mergers and acquisitions for a few months. Things would not fall apart if the vision of corporate growth was put on hold for a few months. Everything would be fine.

Now imagine if all the garbage collectors took the summer off, what would happen? People would have to pile up their garbage in the back yards for the entire hot, stinking summer. Garbage would rot, bugs and rats would come, and there would be more diseases and death in our cities. Eventually there would be a healthcare crisis, and maybe a disease epidemic, all because one group of low prestige people took the summer off. With that in mind, which job is really more valuable to society, the bank president or the garbage collector?

Getting back to the question, though, keep in mind that in a networked economy, every home will be well furnished, so there will be less difference between a mansion and a regular home in a networked economy. In that sense, every home will be very comfortable and perhaps we can all feel like winners. We will all provide a healthy and wealthy lifestyle for our families and ourselves.

We can get over this need to make ourselves feel better with money, though. When we were ruled by monarchies, we used to think that a person with royal blood was more entitled to political rights, like free speech. We got over that. We came to accept that peasants have a right to their opinion, minority religions have a right to practice their faiths, and the press has a right to print the truth even when it is embarrassing to the people in power.

Hopefully we can get over the idea that a person with a lower prestige job has less right to be healthy, to have an education, to eat well, etc. We each have a right to the best that our society has to offer. One of the founding documents of the United States of America, The Declaration of Independence, says that we believe it is self-evident that we all have a right to life, liberty, and the pursuit of happiness. People with less prestigious jobs have a right to pursue their happiness the way they see fit, just like more prestigious people do.

Common comment:	***Many people have the dream of making it rich and retiring young. You are asking people to give that up. If everyone has to work, then nobody is retiring early.***

That is true. Every person would like to have an endless supply of money so that they can live the life of leisure that they always wanted to live. Just like how democracy got rid of the extremes in political power: the slave and the dictator, however, networked capitalism will get rid of the extremes of economic power: poverty and idle wealth. Once upon a time, when we made the transition to democracy from monarchy, some of us had to give up the option of raising an army, conquering some land and creating our own kingdom where our word is law and our power supreme. Now we will have to give up the dream of idle wealth and unlimited economic power. It will be hard for some of us, but it will be better for all of us in the long run.

It is important to note, however, that since any job will provide consumers and their families a comfortable lifestyle, everyone will have nearly unlimited economic power and the ability to do the work that they truly enjoy. So work will not be as much of a burden in a networked economy as it is for some people in a money economy.

When I got out of the Army, I had a job in a wine store/delicatessen and one of the owners of that little store told me one time, “You know Jonathan, if I didn’t have to worry about raising a family and paying the bills, I would just make cabinets. I love working with wood.” And indeed, he was very good at working with things and not very good working with people. Unfortunately, he owned a deli, where he had to interact with people all day. But that is another story.

The point is, many of us have more than one talent, and we will be able to live our dreams much easier in a networked economy. While it is true that we will all have to work and contribute to the economy, we will have the economic power to find the jobs that we truly love, so that working will not be as much of a burden as it is in a money economy.

Common comment: ***Speaking of work, why would a person work hard if they aren't making money?***

Are you saying that the only reason people work hard is for a paycheck? I think it runs a little deeper than that. People will work hard because they will be doing the job that they enjoy most doing. There is an old saying that if you find a job you love, you will never work another day in your life. When any job will earn us and our families a comfortable lifestyle, we can focus on what is really important, which is doing what inspires us. If we find that job that we truly love, we will not want to lose it, because there might not be openings elsewhere in a similar job. So we will work hard.

Keep in mind that people will be able to go wherever they want to go, and businesses will be able to hire the best employees and managers that they can find. Businesses will also have the ability to make their working environments as pleasant as possible at no extra cost or burden. If employees all have the power to get up and walk out at any moment, a business had better treat them well. When people find jobs that they love and the business does its best to make the working environment as good as possible, people will be more than willing to work hard and get the job done.

Common comment: ***What about overtime? What if a project comes up that requires people to work extra hours? How would they be compensated?***

They will work overtime out of loyalty to the company, because they love their work and they do not want to lose that job and risk having to take another job that they like less. OK, stop laughing. There are jobs that people love that much, and places that bring out that level of loyalty. However, if the workplace does not inspire that kind of loyalty, or the work is not the kind of work that anybody really loves, management will just have to give their clients more reasonable projected deadlines, manage production so that sprints in production are not necessary, and perhaps they can hire more people. I suspect, however, that overtime will be a thing of the past when we switch to a networked economy because the employees will not want to work extra hours. Frankly, as we will see, I suspect the opposite will happen. The economy will automate more and more, the work week will become shorter and shorter over time until people spend a few hours working and many hours enjoying their lives.

Common comment:	***How will we be rewarded for working exceptionally hard or doing a great job, if employers can't give their workers bonuses?***

There are many ways to reward someone for doing an exceptional job. They can be given a public award accompanied by some really high praise by the boss. The old "Employee of the Month" award comes to mind. They can also be given a better parking space, a better office, a longer vacation, a promotion, and/or a fancier title to name a few ways. Money is an easy crutch for us in several ways. Bonuses are easy and superficial ways to tell somebody they have done a good job. When we move to a networked economy we will have to find other ways to do some things, including rewarding our best employees, and we will find them.

Common comment:	***And what about mothers? It used to be that a woman could stay home and raise the kids. These days, things are so expensive that both people have to work and the kids suffer not having a parent around. I think you should make an exception for mothers.***

Well, first of all, I am not making the rules and exceptions about anything. I am just throwing the ideas out there. When it comes down to it, local governments will make the laws about the rules for employment and, as we will discuss, the rules for competition between businesses.

But, you are right. Raising and nurturing the next generation is an important job, a valuable contribution to our future. Not just for women, though. There are plenty of men who would enjoy being the person who stays home with the kids. Some writers I know do that very thing right now. That said we should definitely make an exception to the employment requirement for one parent of a school-aged child. If one of the parents wants to stay home and be there for the children, we should enable them to do that. But of course, both parents should be able to work and use daycare to take care of the children if they want to. They should have the flexibility, the economic freedom, to raise their children however they choose.

By the way, we will probably also exclude minors, full time college students, the retired, and the disabled from the employment requirement. Some people are dependents for good reason, obviously, and the economy should support them fully. Students should be able to study or take internships that will help their futures, without worrying about how they are going to eat. Retired folks have already made their contribution to our society and their working days are over. Disabled folks are not able to contribute to the economy and they should be supported as they live out their lives.

Common comment:	***You talked before about people buying what they like. That means a person can buy up all the homes they like. There are only so many of those. That means a few people can buy up all of the land and other people won't have any place to live.***

You are right. Land is a special commodity, since we cannot make more of it ... unless we start shipping people to the moon and the other planets. Once we figure out the demand for land, we might have to set limitations on the amount of residential properties a person can own. Any amount that I wrote would be a guess in the dark. Nations will decide on rules for land ownership for their citizens. Also, I imagine that we will grandfather any limitation to go into effect at sale or inheritance.

Grandfather means that if we transition from a money economy to a networked economy and a limitation is set that a person or married couple can have a maximum of two homes, for example, nobody will have any homes taken away from them at the transition to a networked economy. But, they will not be able to buy or inherit any more homes if they have more homes than the limit allows. So, if a person already owns three properties, they could not buy a fourth property but nobody would take away their property. That way, the real estate limitation will take effect over a generation.

Common comment:	***Then I'd buy a whole mess of property right before we switch over.***

Right. We may have to nullify any over-the-limit purchases that happened for an appropriate period before the transition unless the person can prove that the purchase was normal and reasonable. Once this idea becomes better known and it looks like we are going to network our economy, any purchases might be subject to nullification after we make the transition to a networked economy. Something like that will probably be how it works.

Those are the issues surrounding employment, unlimited acquisition, and private ownership in a networked economy. None of the solutions that I proposed to these issues are set in stone. My goal here is to explore the many issues surrounding the move to a networked economy, and to give the reader an overview. State and local governments around the world will decide on the rules that will apply to their citizens. The basic rule will be that an employed person will earn unlimited access to the economic network for themselves and their dependents. Everything beyond that will vary from one region of the world to the next.

The next section will discuss the definition of employment.

When is a Person Employed?

It is easy to tell when a person is employed in a money economy, because they do something and receive money in exchange. In a networked economy, however, the idea of employment will actually call for some creativity. It is easy to tell when a person is employed when they work for a conventional business that hires them and makes them show up for eight hours a day, five days a week. There are other people, however, who work for themselves doing services for people on a mostly cash basis, who will have to create their own competitive business to be counted as employed.

The real creativity will come, however, when we classify artists, freelance writers, and creative media. When is a painter employed? When is a sculptor employed? Are they employed when they start working on the project? When the work is sold? How long does it count as work after the work is sold? I do not really have a good, issue-resolving, solid answer for this one. In the end, we will probably come up with some compromise.

Perhaps an artist will be required to be sponsored by a museum, and then we will find some measure of minimum public interest based on foot traffic in the museum near their work. The artists that are not good enough to be sponsored by a museum will have to do it as a hobby. Or perhaps independent artists will have to create companies of their own and then have to live up to a standard that requires some minimum amount of demand for their work for their business to maintain its license. Whatever system people can agree on will work as long as it maintains a productive contribution to the economy as a whole.

Proving our Employment

The real issue about employment and a networked economy, though, is how we will communicate to the global economy that a person is indeed employed and therefore deserves full access to the goods and services in the worldwide economic network. In a money economy, people do not care if we have a job, only that we have money. In a networked economy, where the economy is coordinated by a global network, a person will need to prove their status in the network in order for them to acquire things. Throughout the process of designing this new economy I try to use familiar old structures in making new structures. For this task we can use the retail bank and the debit card that we use to take money directly out of our bank accounts to buy goods and services.

Obviously in an economy without money, the banking system will become obsolete. However, it might be transformed instead. The current retail banking system serves people by keeping their money safe and their personal information confidential. We deposit our money with banks knowing that the deposits are safe and the money will be there when we go back for it later. The financial information attached to our accounts, the balance, interest earned and history of deposits and withdrawals is kept confidential by the bank and is accessible by outside people only by court order.

In a networked economy, banks can serve a very similar function. They can serve to keep a person's economic information safe and confidential. In a money economy, an employer often wires their employee's paycheck directly to the bank. The money shows up in the consumer's account without them having to transport the funds to the bank personally. Then, when the consumer wants to buy something, they can use a debit card to pay for the thing with money taken directly out of their bank account.

Similarly, in a networked economy, the employer will send the consumer's bank a monthly notification that, yes, this person is still employed. Then, when the person wants to buy something, they can use a familiar plastic card, resembling a credit card that will be swiped in a machine just like a credit card scanner. The machine will contact the consumer's bank over a network similar to what credit cards use today, and the bank will confirm that the person is employed. With consumer's access to the network verified, the goods will be bagged up and the consumer will be on their way with their new belongings. This will all happen in the same fast, efficient way that credit card transactions happen now.

Using banks as keepers of private employment information will enable the consumer's private information to remain private and enable the economy to keep track of employment.

Some dependents, i.e. children and stay-at-home spouses, rely on their relationship to consumers for their economic power. The banks, therefore, will issue multiple cards to consumers, enough to cover all of the consumer's dependents. People who are retired or permanently disabled will be issued permanent cards for them to use. All of these people will have full access to the economy.

So, that is life in a networked economy for you and me. If we need something, we will go to the store, pick out our items, and take them to the counter. The clerks will scan the items for inventory control. Then, we will give the clerks our bank cards, they will scan them, the network will verify we are either employed or we are dependents of employed people, and we will take our new goods from the store.

Common comment: ***Here is another issue. If I want to go to a concert and I want better seats, I have to pay a higher price for those seats. How can I get those tickets if everyone who wants them can have them?***

Let me answer that question with a question: how do we do that today? It is true that the front row seats to the hottest concerts are more expensive, but there are still plenty of people who will pay those higher prices. How do we determine today who among all the people able to pay the higher price gets the better tickets now? What is the rule?

The rule is "First come, first serve" for things that a whole crowd of people want. If we want tickets to the opening of the latest blockbuster movie, we need to camp out in front of the movie theater.

For things like the Olympics where literally the whole world wants to go, we will just have to get up early and get our orders in as soon as the tickets become available. We will not have to pay more money in a networked economy, but sometimes we will have to pay more diligence and just get there before anyone else.

Unemployment

Common comment:	**_What happens when I lose my job! Are they going to throw me out on the street?_**

No, of course they will not throw you out on the street. The goal for any community, however, is to have as many productive citizens as possible. The more people who work and contribute to the economy, the more goods and services that are available in the market to benefit all of our lives. Also, if people are at work being productive they are not out in the streets getting into trouble. We will need rules that encourage unemployed people to find new jobs as soon as possible, so they are productive.

When a person loses their job, their employer will report the termination to their bank. And when they get a new job, the new employer will send notification to the employee's bank. But what do we do during the period when the consumer is unemployed? In a money economy, the threat of starvation due to the lack of money drives most people to find work, but in a moneyless economy what do we do about unemployment and how do we deal with people who do not want to work?

We can set up employment agencies, using the current network of public employment agencies. These agencies will be networked and every employer who has an open position will list their openings with the public network. That will provide a nice central place for people to look for work in their hometown or across the globe.

Local governments will have to decide on their rules for unemployment. After a person becomes unemployed, their local government could give them a period of time to look for a new job, requiring them to be active in the public network of job listings. I am tempted to name a flat time-period, like six months, for example, to look for work.

Common comment: ***But then people would work for a month and then "lose" their jobs, and take half a year to find another job. Then they would work for another few weeks, "lose" their job again, and take another long vacation.***

Right. So, that will not work. The period of allowed unemployment will have to be short for short periods of employment. Maybe the rule could enable a period of up to six months or half the time they were employed if they worked for less than a year. That way, if they worked four months, they would have only two months to look for a job. Then if they cannot find a job, they will have to take whatever they can find or be cut off from the system. Alternatively, the local government could require them to work in local hospitals, police stations, *etc.* and contribute to the local community. They can continue to look for their dream job while they do a less-than-dreamy job. There has to be a point, though, where if a person will not work, they are just cut off. There has to be some consequences for refusing to contribute to the economy, and we have to use our self-interested nature to drive people to work hard.

The actual rules and time frames that the local government chooses are really arbitrary. Whatever people agree on will work, and the rules will evolve over time as local areas experiment with different sets of rules. We all need to be productive, though, and the rules should encourage that.

* * *

The point to this section, though, is that we can manage a complex economy without money. Employment will enable full access to the global economy and we will link local banks around the world to keep track of employment and make sure that our population is as productive as possible. Our dependents will be excused from the employment requirement. Opening up the economy to the full force of total human demand will put pressure on the economy to increase production and use the full resources of the environment to meet our needs. Taking away the money requirement will also abolish poverty worldwide, as everyone will have access to the economy for the first time in human history.

Using employment as the access requirement to a networked economy will enable us to fulfill the needs of both the population and the needs of the economy. Money capitalism fulfills the needs of the economy, providing workers to make products for those of us who have money, without worrying too much about the needs of the whole population. Utopian dreams of communism and anarchy talk about fulfilling the needs of the population while disregarding the needs of an advanced economy. For the first time in human history, we can both maintain a vibrant, competitive economy, and enable every person to take full advantage of that economy.

Of course we have not discussed competition between businesses. That is where it gets really interesting.

Chapter 3

Competing without Money

Networked Capitalist Competition

To start a business in a money economy, in the United States anyway, potential business owners file the incorporation papers with the state department of corporations, and they take their business plan to the bank to get a business loan so that they can lease or buy space, inventory and supplies. Then, they advertise and promote the business to draw in customers. As long as they sell enough products to pay the business loan, supplies, the overhead on whatever space they rent, the salaries of their employees, their own salaries, and whatever ongoing advertising they use, they stay in business. If the sales start to drop, they have to find ways to cut back spending without killing the business and they innovate to increase sales. This goes on until they get to a point where things pick up or they just have to close the business.

Starting a business in a networked economy will be a lot like it is in a money economy. New businesses will register themselves with the state, receive their license, and then open up shop. The local and state governments, who will maintain the rules of competition will want to give new businesses a certain period of time to establish themselves and attract customers, so they might give the business a year before they will have to live up to the rules of competition. During this trial period the new business will have unlimited access to the economic network and unlimited power to advertise themselves and make their services known to potential consumers. At the end of the year, if they cannot attract the minimum number of customers or sell the minimum number of products, they might be given an additional year's probation to enable them to get their sales up before they will lose their license.

To measure competition, the economy will once again use an existing institution, what are now the state and federal tax collection agencies, to collect and publish sales information for businesses.

We might rename the tax agencies Competition Measurement Offices ("CMOs"). These offices will function as a kind of accounting office, collecting data and publishing the results. They will have no control over which businesses succeed or fail, save one power that they will need to have over the rules of competition in the beginning when we are implementing the new economy, which we will discuss shortly.

Before a business starts in a networked economy, the owner will register the business with the appropriate CMO depending on where they want to compete for customers. It was mentioned earlier that in a networked economy, businesses will compete for the number of units sold or customers served, and a business will have to maintain a certain minimum level of sales to keep its accreditation and have access to the network of distributors. If a person opens a local business, they will not want to compete with national brands for number of units sold. Therefore local businesses will compete with local businesses, regional businesses with regional businesses, national with national, and international businesses will compete only with other similar international businesses.

The state CMO will define and measure competition for each particular geographic area of competition within that state, whether it is a particular rural town, a county, a metropolitan area, or the state as a whole. The federal CMO will define and measure competition in larger areas like regions of the country or the nation as a whole. There will also be an international CMO for international businesses. The new business owner will choose where they want to compete. As a business grows, they will need to register with the higher level CMO as appropriate.

For example, if I wanted to own a hardware store, I would want to compete within my home city for customers. I would register with the state CMO as a hardware store within my home city and the CMO would send me the rules of competition that I would have to live up to in order to keep my business license. Then, if I decide to expand my services and open stores in other parts of the state, I would notify the CMO and would have to compete under the rules for statewide hardware chains. Then if I expanded out of the state, I would have to register with the federal CMO and compete based on the rules for regional hardware chains. If I expanded beyond my region, I would have to compete against other national hardware chains.

Common comment:	***Wait a minute! The government is going to set the rules of competition! Nobody wants some bureaucrat telling them how to run their business!***

You are right. That is why the government will not make the rules. This economy will be run by the people for the people. The rules will be set by the businesses that are competing against each other. Nobody knows the market like the people who are competing within that market, so when the new economy is being implemented, each industry will get together and set the rules that it will compete by.

Common comment:	***That's even worse! The businesses will make the rules so easy that nobody will ever go out of business. We will have a stagnant economy with no real competition!***

That is where we come to the one power that the Competition Measurement Offices will need to have. When networked capitalism is being set up, each type of business will submit its rules to their CMO, which will approve or disapprove the rules the businesses decide on. If their CMO rejects the rules, the businesses will have to come back with new rules.

Common comment:	***By what standard will these bureaucrats decide?***

The rules should be tough enough so that useless businesses are forced to close but easy enough so that the rules do not benefit just the most popular businesses. A competitive economy needs a market that is tight enough to inspire spirited competition and loose enough so that new competitors can enter the market. After the implementation period, the rules will be set for that type of business in that market. Of course a business will be able to ask the CMO to look at the rules again later if the business thinks the market has changed and the rules are no longer fair or appropriate. So, choosing a market will involve some strategy for a new business, depending on the existing rules of competition and what businesses already exist in that market, both of which will be publicly available.

Example of Networked Competition

Now for an example set of rules. Imagine a group of five bookstores which make up the bookstore market of a large town. They will compete based on the number of books sold, which is easy to measure. Here in no particular order is a list of the stores, their average sales per month, and market share based on their raw sales:

Bookstore Market in Town X

Name	Average Book Sales per Month	Market Share (%)
Book Crooks	52	0.29
Sewer Books	988	5.48
Towers O' Paper	8,941	49.62
Book Worm	762	4.23
Great Books	7,278	40.39
Total	18,021	100.00

As we can see, two businesses, "Towers O' Paper" and "Great Books", dominate the local market with ninety percent of the market between them. Then two smaller stores, "Sewer Books" and "Book Worm", do less business, around four or five percent of the market. Finally, there is a small shop "Book Crooks" that does hardly any business at all. The goal here is to create dynamic competition between these five bookstores.

The simplest option would be to create some minimum number of books that the stores would have to sell to keep their business license. For instance, they might set the number at 250 books per month average over a one year period. This would exclude "Book Crooks", which looks like it may be some kind of criminal front company anyway. This is a minimum number and it shows that if a store meets this minimum, it has some value to the economy.

Common comment: ***But, that's not competition! That's just some low bar minimum.***

Exactly right. We want the businesses to fight to give customers the best service and the best products. The rules need to set the businesses against each other, so that one's gain is another's loss.

Common comment:	***And you can't use the number of books sold, because the market will change from one year to the next. Two hundred fifty books might look like a lot now, but it might not be down the road. You want rules that last.***

So the best thing to do is to use market share and …

Common Comment:	***But if employees are free to a business and if the only measure of success is the share of the market, then I would hire myself as many employees as possible and serve the heck out of my customers. Then I would be the best store.***

Right, and that is why…

Common Comment:	***Then you would have an economy full of fat businesses with a whole bunch of people standing around doing nothing, because they will all hire as many people as possible!***

Exactly! It would be competitive but not productive! So, sure, "Towers O' Paper" above sells almost nine thousand books a month, but how many people does it take to sell those books? We want the economy to do as much as possible with as little labor as possible. We want these stores to sell as many books as possible for each hour of labor they get from their employees. And that is the key to having a productive economy without using money.

We can call each hour of labor used a "labor hour" and use that as a unit of productivity. So if a business is open for an hour and ten people are working in the store for that hour, the store used ten labor hours to stay open for that hour. How many books did they sell in that hour using those ten labor hours? That will be their book sales per labor hour and that is how we can measure productivity without money. What is the average number of sales for the month per labor hour? How ever many books they sold divided by the ten labor hours used, will be their books sold per labor hour for that hour of business.

For this example we will assume that all labor is created equal and we will count an hour that the boss works at the same value as an hour that the newest stock person works. So, now we have to figure out how many labor hours each of those stores used and how many sales they made for each of those labor hours. Are you still with me?

Common Comment:	***Uh, yeah. I got it. If I owned the store, I would need to sell these books, but with as few employees as possible. So, instead of dollars per hour, I would think of them as sales per hour. I need to hire people who would do the most to increase my sales. If they aren't increasing my sales, they are pulling me back. I need to keep those people to as few as possible; the ones that pull my sales per labor hour back. Sounds like capitalism. I got it.***

Good. Here is a new table that includes the number of employees, the total number of employee hours worked, and the average number of books sold in a month for each hour. I assume part-time employees work exactly twenty hours a week and full time employees work exactly forty hours a week. So each full time person puts in forty hours a week, times fifty two weeks in a year, divided by twelve to find the monthly average labor hours. Part time people work twenty hours a week, times fifty two weeks, and divided by twelve to find the monthly average hours. We can combine these averages to find the total average labor hours that the stores use. Basically, we want to know how many units are sold for each hour that a person works.

Bookstore Market in Town X

Name	Average Book Sales per Month	Employees: Total	Employees: Full Time	Employees: Part Time	Total Labor Hours/ Month	Sales Per Labor Hour	Market Share Per Labor Hour (%)
Book Crooks	52	4	2	2	520	0.1	1
Sewer Books	988	15	4	11	1,646	0.6	9
Towers O' Paper	8,941	35	8	27	3,725	2.4	34
Book Worm	762	6	2	4	693	1.1	16
Great Books	7,278	25	5	20	2,599	2.8	40
Total	18,021					7.0	100

Measuring the market share based on sales per hour worked really shows the value of the business to the economy. Notice that in the earlier table, "Towers O' Paper" had the most market share, but when we add in productivity, we see that "Great Books" is actually the market leader since they have fewer people per sale. Also the two second tier stores looked before like they were about the same value to the economy, but adding in productivity enables "Book Worm" to really leap ahead. "Sewer Books" has a lot more employees. This way of measuring competition is also important because it enables small stores to compete with big stores. A small mom-and-pop store with just them working may not sell a lot of books, but if it is just the two of them working, they may have a leading market share because they would be very productive.

Common Comment: Am I going to have to know how to calculate all of that?

Not necessarily. The calculation of productive market share is for the eggheads like me who really want to calculate this stuff. Most people will not have to know that any more than they know in a money economy how to calculate the price of an option contract in investments. All you will need to know is that if you have a business, you will need to sell as much product with as little labor as possible. If you do not own a business, all you need to know is that if you have a job, you can buy whatever you need. If you are old enough to retire, you would not even have to know that. Just buy what you need and thanks for everything you have done in the past when you did work.

In addition, because we account for productivity in networked capitalism and make businesses compete only with other similar businesses, this system automatically adjusts for different industries, because while one person could really run a book store, other industries are more labor intensive. If a business requires a certain amount of administration, or a large package handling system for example, all of their competitors will have the same requirements. That is why we compare similar businesses, because each competitor has the same structural requirements as their competitors. So, the businesses will compete not only for selling the most goods and services, but also they will compete over who can prepare, handle, and sell those goods and services in the most efficient way.

Common Comment: ***I'd get machines to do as much of the work as possible. That way I would need fewer people to do the work.***

Exactly. Networked capitalism will also encourage automation. In a money economy, a lot of people think that buying a machine takes a job away from a person, which is less money in the person's pocket. In a networked economy, however, more machines are a good thing. They free up the employees to do less menial jobs, without taking any food off their tables.

Designing the Rules

So, how do we develop rules that will set these businesses against each other and provide their customers with the best products and the best service? We could require a minimum market share relative to the market leader. "Sewer Books" above serves 9 percent of the market demand while "Great Books" serves 40 percent of the market demand. Nine is 22.5 percent of 40. The rule when the network is being set up could be that each business must maintain a market share equal to or greater than 20 percent of the market leader's market share. So, for this market at this time, the minimum required market share is 8 percent (twenty percent of 40). Here is the table again.

Bookstore Market in Town X

Name	Average Book Sales per Month	Employees			Total Labor Hours/ Month	Sales Per Labor Hour	Market Share Per Labor Hour (%)
		Total	Full Time	Part Time			
Book Crooks	52	4	2	2	520	0.1	1
Sewer Books	988	15	4	11	1,646	0.6	9
Towers O' Paper	8,941	35	8	27	3,725	2.4	34
Book Worm	762	6	2	4	693	1.1	16
Great Books	7,278	25	5	20	2,599	2.8	40
Total	18,021					7.0	100

Those market rules will knock out "Book Crooks", who should be having a hard time paying four people with only 52 book sales a month anyway. Maybe they are very rare, expensive books. Maybe the business is a front for criminal activity. If the store is open six days a week, they sell only two books a day. If those rules are accepted, "Book Crooks" will have a year to increase their market share, before they will lose their accreditation. This may seem unfair, but we need a productive economy. We cannot have four people standing around selling two books a day. If the owners of the business like to trade rare books, perhaps this is more of a hobby than a business, like selling things on EBay.com. They could do this in their spare time while working at another job.

Each increase in sales or decrease in the number of people employed by a store will increase their market share and decrease the market leader's market share. If a business brings down the market share for the leader, it lowers the bar for everyone, since the required market share is a percentage of the market leader. For example, the current minimum market share is 8 percent. If "Towers O' Paper" fired 5 part-time workers, it would increase their market share from 34 percent to 37 percent and knock "Great Books'" market share back to 38 percent, which would lower the minimum required market share to 7.6 percent (twenty percent of 38). Every little bit counts in business. Here is the new picture of their competition:

Revised Bookstore Market in Town X

Name	Average Book Sales per Month	Employees: Total	Employees: Full Time	Employees: Part Time	Total Labor Hours/ Month	Sales Per Labor Hour	Market Share Per Labor Hour (%)
Book Crooks	52	4	2	2	520	0.1	1
Sewer Books	988	15	4	11	1,646	0.6	9
Towers O' Paper	8,941	30	8	22	3,725	2.7	37
Book Worm	762	6	2	4	693	1.1	16
Great Books	7,278	25	5	20	2,599	2.8	38
Total	18,021					7.3	100

If one store innovates and improves its share of the market, other stores will have to innovate as well to keep up. If overall demand for books falls, the businesses will have to scramble to keep up their share of the smaller total demand. Less customer traffic could mean fewer needed employees, or maybe they will decide to add another business line, like a café in the bookstore, or maybe they will decide to bring in local writers to conduct readings in the store. Since all of the stores will have the same unlimited economic power to buy whatever they need to innovate or advertise, the boundaries of the competition will be the limits of the managers' imaginations. That could get very interesting.

The rule for these businesses in this market is that every book store must maintain a "sales-per-labor-hour" market share of at least 20 percent of the market leader. That rule would stay the same until the rule is changed with their CMO. Over time the market may change, with overall demand increasing or diminishing, the city growing or shrinking, and the population changing. Occasionally, the rules of competition will need to change to fit the changing reality of the market. So, if a new business petitioned the CMO complaining that the rules were too tight to enable new business a fair chance to break into the market, for example, the CMO might review the rules and ask the competitors to revise the rules.

Not every region will have the same rules for a particular industry of course. Each local area will determine their own rules and each local CMO will use their own standards to make sure the rules are not too strict or too loose. As the networked market is being set up and the rules of competition are being established, there will be all of the usual political lobbying trying to influence the guidelines that the CMO will follow in deciding which rules are too strict or too relaxed. Different states and regions will create rules based on their own cultural and societal priorities.

For simplicity in the previous example, I assumed that all hours worked were created equal. Businesses might want to get more complicated, though. For example they could account for the increased productivity of seniority by dividing the number of hours a person works by the number of years the person has worked in their industry. Therefore, for the purposes of calculating productivity an hour worked by a new person will be equal to a half hour worked by a person who had been there two years, and equal to three minutes worked by someone who had been in the industry for twenty years. (1 hour, or sixty minutes, divided by 20 is three minutes)

For the purposes of calculating market share, assuming all full time people work forty hours per week, a full time new person will work forty hours per week and that would equal forty labor hours. But a twenty year veteran could work forty hours and it will only count as if he had worked 2 labor hours per week. (Forty divided by twenty equals two) That seems fair and it will make more senior people more valuable to the business, because their labor is assumed to be more productive. And there will surely be other innovations that I have not thought of. This is an area, refining the measure of productivity to accurately reflect the value of different types of labor, where the economists of the world will be very interested and very active.

Common Comment: So what if I am the only book store in town? What will be my rules of competition then?

Another great question: what if you are the only business like yours in town? That can happen in small towns. Or what if you are a new kind of business that nobody has thought of yet? Or what if you are a business with a product that is very hard to measure? A university for example has a service that is easy to measure, teaching, but many would argue that it's more valuable service is research, which is much harder to measure.

In cases where competition is hard to measure either because it does not exist or because the product of the business is just too hard to convert into numbers, the local Competition Measurement Office can measure a business' required minimum production based on its capacity. A business might be required to function above some minimum capacity for the facilities that it has and the number of people that it employs.

The only bookstore in town, for example, might have to function in line with academic estimates on the maximum number of books it could sell if its employees worked constantly. If a person were constantly ringing up customers, with whatever the average number of books customers purchase at the register, how many books is it humanly possible to rings up, including the time it takes to greet the customer, bag the sale, etc? How much time does it take a stock person to shelve books and what is the maximum number of books that he could stock in a work day? They might add up all of these store functions and determine the maximum capacity of books sold for each labor hour for each employee employed. Then, the CMO may require the business to fulfill a certain percent of that capacity for the number of employees it has, maybe seventy percent, although that sounds a little high.

Universities likewise may be required to maintain a student population that is at least ninety percent of its capacity, and produce research at a pace per researcher that is at least the average for researchers in each academic field. I pulled those numbers out of thin air, of course; the local CMOs will make decisions based on individual circumstances and research for productive capacity across the particular industry that the business belongs to. As we approach implementation, researchers who study industrial systems will develop maximum capacity estimates for each industry and competition measurement offices will use those estimates to create their rules for competition.

Common Comment: ***You said that the one store could increase its market share by firing a few of its part time workers. That rang a bell for me because people work part time usually for extra money. In a moneyless economy, will there even be part time workers?***

No, there probably would not, actually. I used part time workers to make that example more realistic, but you are right. Part time workers are often otherwise dependent on someone for their livelihood, like students, retired folks, or stay-at-home parents. In a networked economy, there would be no reason for them to work, so they would not. That is getting a little ahead of the discussion, though. I will talk more about that when I talk about how society will be different in a networked economy.

Common Comment:	***Now that I think of it, without money what will be the motivation for even starting a business? If there is no money, no profit, why will someone start a business? I can't see how someone will go through the hassle of starting a business if they didn't get something out of it.***

Not many people start a business just to get rich, even people who start large businesses. And if they do think they will get rich, they soon find out otherwise. People who just want to be rich usually just want the life of leisure that they think comes with being rich, but running a business is not easy. Most business owners work fifty- to eighty hour weeks for a middle class lifestyle. Maybe after decades of hard work, opening more than one location and hiring managers to take over operations, a business owner might find themselves living the good life. That is a long road, though.

Some people start a business because they are the type of person who just cannot work for other people. Others could work for other people but they really want to run their own show. Some inventive people have an amazing idea and they want to see if it will work. That is why I am writing this book. I have an amazing idea that I just cannot keep inside any longer, so I am creating a product to sell to people, telling them about it. Other people just like running businesses, creating a product, feeling the thrill of public approval when people really like their product, and of course beating the pulp out of their competitors. All of those things will still exist in a networked economy; they just will not be expressed as money.

Actually, I believe that in an economy without the risk of poverty for a failed entrepreneur more people will take the leap and open their own businesses. There are many people in this world who would like to own their own business and do what they love to do, but the reality is too daunting. Perhaps they do not understand the financial aspects about how to get the space, the supplies and the financing. Perhaps they do not want to take the risk.

A good friend of mine for example is a wonderful photographer and she loves taking pictures. She could make a great living behind the lens. People whose weddings she has photographed have told her they already had inquiries and they could send her business. But she just does not do it; she does administrative work for a construction company. There is nothing wrong with administrative work, but it is not what she loves. But do not worry; there will be plenty of new businesses in a networked economy.

Common Comment:	***OK, here's another problem. I got you! I found the flaw. This whole economy is coordinated through the internet, right?***

Right.

Common Comment:	***So what will we do if the electricity fails? You can't use the internet if the electricity goes out. Money works day and night, anywhere, whether the lights are on or not.***

Ah! Where will we be when the lights go out? Consumers will need a way to verify their employment when they go into stores during a blackout or in the case of a catastrophe. To tackle this problem we will convert another money-related structure, the paycheck, into a non-money related structure, the employment card.

Instead of the paycheck or paystub that our employers hand us every two weeks, employers will give their employees a wallet-sized paper card each month with the business' federal employer identification number and the employee's information on it, verifying employment. The employee and their dependents will keep these cards in their wallets and purses. If there is a blackout, merchants can take down that information and enable people who have a recently dated card to buy what they need from the store. Then, when the electricity comes back on, the merchant can upload that information to their CMO manually.

Competition measurement offices could distribute receipt forms to merchants with little circles to fill in customer information and item numbers like they use on standardized examinations. During the blackout, the merchant would have customers fill these out listing the customer information and what the customer bought. The merchant would file these forms and mail them to their CMO, where the forms can be run through a computerized reader to download the information and measure their market share.

Actually, once the system is in place, the networked economy could run completely without electricity, assuming everyone kept ledgers. Employers could give their employees a paper card every month to show employment. Merchants could record each transaction with the goods and the consumer's identification number listed on these receipt forms and then in a ledger. Then, weekly, the merchant could send ledger summaries and standardized forms to their competition measurement office via the postal service.

The CMO would add up demand, and calculate market share. The CMO could send out auditors periodically to make sure the summaries match the merchants' ledgers. If a producer fell below his minimum market share, the CMO could notify the producer's wholesalers via regular mail. So, this economy does not actually need the internet to work, but anyone can see the non-internet version is a whole lot of paperwork being shuffled back and forth. The internet enables instantaneous, worldwide coordination. This shows however, that even with an extended loss of electricity, the networked economy could be maintained. This kind of back-up system could be kept in reserve to be used in case of attack or other catastrophe.

* * *

So, there you are. That is how we manage a complex, dynamic, capitalist economy without a money commodity that gets in the way of our dreams, complicates our lives, and fluctuates wildly in value, causing inflation, recessions, depressions, and widespread misery. For you and me, life will be much simpler. We will have to work to contribute to the economic network, just like we do now, but otherwise it will be like using a credit card with no limit to pay for everything, and then never paying the bill. All of the things we need and want will be available to us, whether it is food, housing, entertainment, healthcare, education or whatever.

Each state and province around the world will create a competition measurement office, where local businesses will register their rules and compete for consumer patronage based on the number of goods and services they sell. Each nation will create a national competition measurement office for regional and nationwide businesses, and there will be an international office for international businesses. There will be a network similar to our existing credit card network, where businesses around the world can contact a consumer's local bank to verify their employment and then enable the consumer to take home anything they want or need. Life will be amazingly similar to how it is now for affluent people. For everyone else, they will get to be affluent themselves.

We can create a diagram to show how we all fit into a money economy:[14]

Economic Distribution in a Money Economy

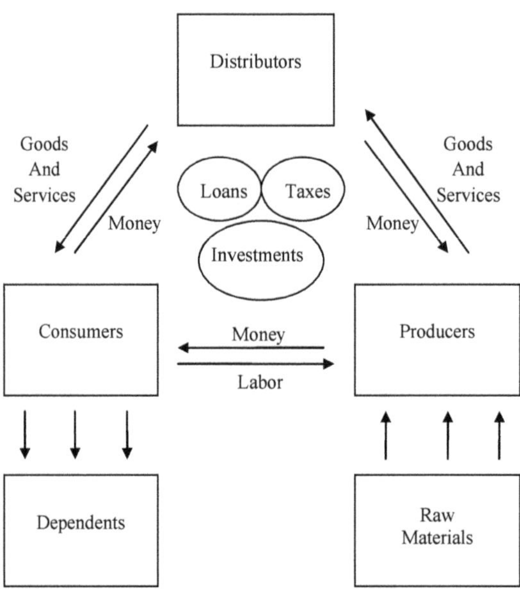

As we can see, consumers trade their labor for money, which is combined with raw materials from the environment to produce goods and services that are ultimately sold back to consumers through distributors.[15] The diagram is not perfect, of course, since consumers also sell their labor

---

[14] In creating this diagram, I adapted Joseph Schumpeter's description of the 'basic process of economic life' (1956, pp. 150-153). That contributed what he calls the 'circular flow of production expenditure and consumption', and I utilized Helferrich's differentiation between production, consumption and distribution to describe the interactions (1927, p. 308). I then added the fourth actor, the dependent, and the three intervening institutions: loans, investments and taxes. See also Simmel, 1907, p. 469, for an interesting analogy between money's role in capitalism and the role of blood in the body; also Parsons and Smelser, 1956, p. 71 for a discussion about the interactions between producers and consumers that is loosely similar to the above.

[15] Helferrich, 1927, p. 308; Gansmann, 1988, p. 304

to distributors, and producers also sell their goods and services directly to consumers, but for the sake of simplicity, and symmetry, this is how I represent the economy. The economy is a vast matrix of exchange that I have tried to represent in its simplest form for the sake of illustration.

Loans, taxes, and investments also affect the money supply that consumers, producers and distributors can use to carry on economic trade. Taxes decrease our money supply in the short term, but contribute to a stable business environment and long term prosperity, assuming the government spends the taxes well. Loans increase our money supply in the short term but must be paid back with interest over time. So, if we are wise we use the loans for purposes that will make us more money over time than the interest rate will cost us. Investments subtract from our money supply in the short term and hopefully increase our money supply over the long term, assuming they are used well and the investments make money.

Here is a modified diagram showing how the networked economy will work:

Economic Distribution in a Networked Economy

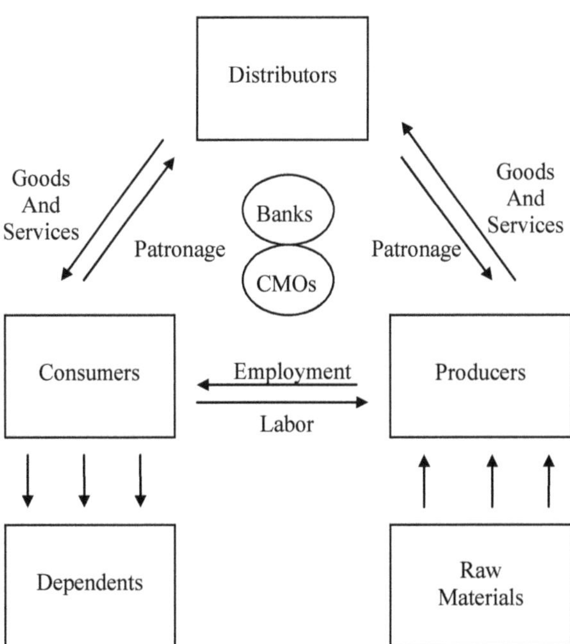

Producers will take raw materials from the environment, combine them with labor from consumers and create products to sell to other consumers. Money of course has been taken out of the network of exchange and replaced with the information that each person and business needs to prove their value to the economy. Producers and distributors need patronage from other businesses and consumers to show the amount of market demand their products and services satisfy. Consumers need employment information to show that their skills are in demand by the economy. Dependents still get what they need without contributing to the economy. Banks and CMOs will measure exchange and communicate our contribution to the various members of the economy.

Would This Really Work?

With the networked economy outlined, the next question is, "Would this really work?" This is a very important question, because if it would not work, there is no reason to do it. Let us break that question down into two smaller questions: "Is this an economy?" and "Is this economy democratic?"

Is this an Economy? This is an important question, because we need to know that the system we have designed does everything that an economy is supposed to do. Nigel Dodd, a distinguished senior lecturer with the London School of Economics, analyzed the role that the monetary network serves in our economy. Since we want to replace that network, the networked economy should perform all of the same functions that the monetary network fulfills. Here are Dodd's five abstract properties of a monetary network:

1. "The network will contain a standardized accounting system into which each monetary form within the network is divisible, enabling its exchange with anything priced in terms of that system."
2. "Money is accepted as payment almost solely on the assumption that it can be re-used later on."
3. "The network will depend on information regarding its spatial characteristics: limits placed on the territory in which" it can be used.
4. "The network is based on legalistic information, usually in the form of rules."

5. "Anyone in possession of money must be able to anticipate, as a matter of routine, its re-use" with other people across the territory.[16]

How does the networked economy match up?

First, does the new economy include a standardized accounting system that enables the exchange of any good or service? Yes. The network has a mechanism for including every person, either as a working consumer, or the dependent of a working consumer, in the economy. Any business can register with their local competition measurement office to hire employees to create their goods and services, and to offer their goods and services to the public. There is no limitation placed on what goods and services can be offered to the public, other than the fact that they must be legal to possess and exchange. No illegal drugs, heavy firearms, or weapons of mass destruction.

Second, can people trust that the method of exchange will be available today, tomorrow, next year and beyond? Yes. Once the system is set up, it will be enforced and maintained by the governments of the world, just as the money system is maintained today. Of course the governments' role in maintaining the economy will be severely diminished when there are no more taxes to collect and redistribute, financial institutions to regulate and inspect, or interest rates to monitor and adjust. The government's economic role will be reduced to the role of accountant, adding up sales data, determining market share, and publishing the results. That will be performed mostly at the state and local level. The federal government will be almost entirely removed from the economy. However, people will have full faith that the system will last when it is backed by the full faith and support of the world community.

Third, will there be clear information about the spatial limitations of the networked economy? Yes. Businesses will know their rules of competition, which will be determined and maintained by each local area. As businesses expand to cover larger areas, they will have to register with the larger competition measurement office. Individuals will have spatial limitations about where they can buy what they need from the economy only if there are nations that choose not to network their economies. Every nation that is on the economic network will fully benefit its citizens and enable them to acquire whatever they need.

---

[16] Dodd, 1994, p. xxiv. Dalton, 1971, pp. 1-25 provides a similar typology.

Fourth, will the network consist of clear rules that carry the weight of law to determine how economic exchange will take place? Yes. The rules for employment, unemployment, and competition between businesses will be determined and enforced by local governments. Those rules will be clearly communicated to everyone.

Fifth, will people be able to trust that they will be able to acquire what they need from any business in the network across town, across the country, and across the world? Yes. Every person will be to get what they need from every business in every nation around the globe.

Is it Democratic? Networked capitalism looks like it will do all of the things that an economy is supposed to do. Will the new networked economy be democratic? Will it be a fair distribution of economic power that will benefit every person in the society? Luckily the eminent political scientist from Yale University, Robert Dahl outlined what a democratic distribution of power within an association of people would look like. Of course he was talking about government and we are talking about economics, so here is a guide for converting from one to the other:

Policies = Products
Votes = Purchases
Association = Economy
Agenda = Marketplace
Adoption = Deemed a Success

The economic word is in brackets to help the reader understand how this applies to economics.

1. *Effective Participation.* Before a policy [product] is adopted [deemed a success] by the association [economy], all the members must have equal and effective opportunities for making their views known to the other members as to what the policy [product] should be.

2. *Voting [Purchasing] Equality.* When the moment arrives at which the decision about a policy [product] will finally be made, every member must have an equal and effective opportunity to vote [purchase], and all votes [purchases] must be counted as equal.

3. *Enlightened Understanding.* Within reasonable limits as to time, each member must have equal and effective opportunities for learning about the relevant alternative policies [products] and their likely consequences.
4. *Control of the Agenda [Marketplace].* The members must have the exclusive opportunity to decide how and, if they choose, what matters [products] are to be placed on the agenda [marketplace]. Thus the democratic process required by the three preceding criteria is never closed. The policies [products] of the association [economy] are always open to change by the members, if they so choose.
5. *Inclusion of Adults.* All, or at any rate most, adult permanent residents should have the full rights of citizens that are implied by the first four criteria.[17]

Will networked capitalism be democratic?

First, before a product is deemed a success or failure, will every member of the community have the equal opportunity to purchase that item if they choose? In other words, when a business is created and a good or service is offered to the marketplace, will every person be able to buy that product if they choose? Yes. Businesses will have at least one year to establish themselves within the marketplace before they have to live by the rules of competition for their area. Also, every person will have unlimited economic power to buy what they want from the economy.

Second, will every purchase be counted equally when determining which products succeed and which products fail? Yes. Every purchase will be added up, and counted only once, to determine an overall level of sales for that product. Those sales will be compared to the sales of other similar products to determine the market share for each product.

Third, will every person have enough time to learn about various products in the marketplace, and buy whichever products they prefer before the products are deemed a success or failure? Yes. Every business will have at least one year to make themselves known in the marketplace and every consumer will have that time to learn about new products and decide whether or not to purchase them.

---

[17] Dahl, 1998, pp. 37-38.

Fourth, will the market be open to new products and will every person have the ability to bring a new product to the marketplace if they choose? Yes. Every person will have the economic power to create a business and offer whatever products they choose to the marketplace. Starting a business will be free, as will buying the inventory to stock the business. Every person in the world economic network will be completely free to bring their products to the marketplace and then remove those products when they choose.

The second part of this point is if the community decides that they no longer like a product, is there a mechanism for the product to be removed from the marketplace? Yes. Businesses will have to maintain a particular share of their market. As long as a business attracts enough consumers, they will be able to keep their business license and maintain access to the network of suppliers that they need to stock their businesses. If consumers do not patronize the business, the business will lose their license and lose access to the network, and they will be unable to acquire the supplies needed to keep their business running. It is up to consumers to maintain support for a given product, or withdraw that support and force it to close. Therefore, consumers will have equal and exclusive control over the marketplace.

Fifth, will every adult have access to the marketplace and be equally able to exercise the four previous rights? Yes. Not only will every adult have full and equal access to the economy, but every person of every age will have access by their status as either an employed person or a dependent of an employed person, or a dependent of the state for disabled or institutionalized consumers. Dependents will include children, the retired, the disabled, and one parent of a school-aged child.

Therefore, by these measurements, not only will this absolutely work, but I have created the holy grail of economic innovations: a stable, competitive, democratic economy that will benefit everyone and adapt to the changing needs of the society. Reformers and revolutionaries have been seeking economic democracy for hundreds of years and thanks to the invention of the internet and its instantaneous, global communication of value, economic democracy, i.e. universally equal economic freedom, is finally possible for the human race.

Next, we will talk about how we will transition from a money economy to a networked economy.

Chapter 4

The Transition from Money Capitalism to Networked Capitalism

How do we get there from here? What step by step process can we take to slowly and steadily move from a money economy to a networked economy? The networked economy is an alternative accounting system that can be set up along side of the money economy and tested while the money economy is still being used. The networked economy will not disturb the money economy while it is being tested. This is a great benefit to the economy as I have designed it, because obviously we cannot just throw away our money and TA-DA! There we are! We must put the networked economy into place and test it over a few years before we stop using money.

Also, this idea is not completely developed. This book is just the introduction to the idea, the beginning of the conversation. There is a great deal of work left to do:

1. We have to overcome the many obstacles that exist to implementing networked capitalism. There are social obstacles, political obstacles, and technological obstacles to moving toward a networked economy.

2. We need to do more research to determine how much people will consume when they can consume anything. A key to making networked capitalism work is balancing the amount of goods that we take from nature with both the demands of the population and the amount of demand that the environment can sustainably support.

3. Before we can begin implementing the new economy, we will need a simple software program to run the system that is

universal enough to be used with any language and any culture in the world.

4. Legislatures will rewrite their criminal codes to create non-money penalties for minor violations. Many minor violations proscribe a money fine, which obviously cannot be paid in an economy where money does not exist.

5. Local governments will create the Bank/CMO network to keep track of and communicate employment, supply and demand. Once we create that network, businesses around the world will create the rules that they will compete under, and CMOs around the world will review all of those sets of rules for each type of business in each market.

6. Banks will collect information about their customers' dependents and then issue bank cards to their customers and their customers' dependents and educate them on how to use them.

7. We will need to test the system, running it along side of the money economy for at least two or three years to work out any bugs.

8. When the networked economy is fully tested as a ghost system running along side the money economy, and we decide to really transition to a networked economy, producers around the world will need to increase production to meet the increased demand that people will have when they can buy anything.

9. When everything is in place and tested, stores have the increased inventory to handle the increased demand, and everyone knows what is going to happen, we will discontinue the money economy.

However, before we go through that whole process on the global scale, we should set it up and test it in one small nation with the whole world providing the test nation with all of the goods and services it demands. Then if the new economy does not work for whatever reason, the world can help that nation move back to a money economy. If it does work, we can begin changing the world. This is a diagram of the implementation process:

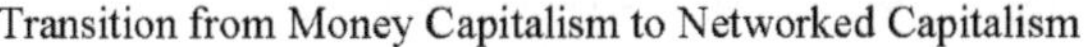

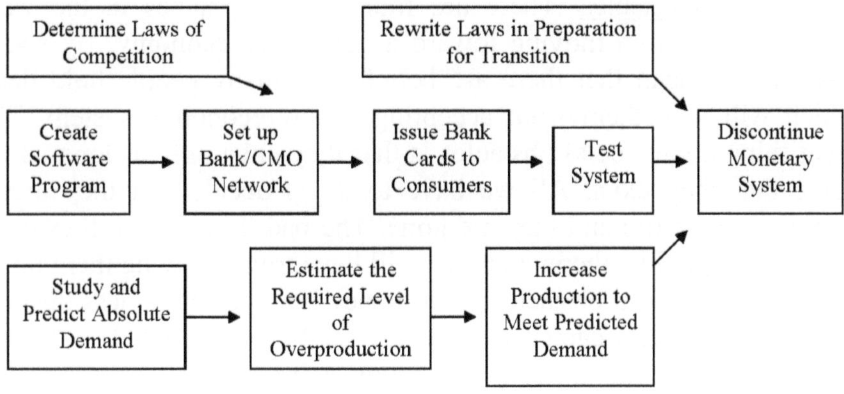

Common Comment: Wow! That's complicated! How long will that take?

It may take a long time for people in all 200 or so nations on the planet to learn about this idea and decide to give it a try. Although it could be undertaken by a block of nations who have the resources to create an economic network with everything their populations need. However, once we finally get to the point where we start the transition, it will take at least ten years, but probably closer to twenty years to complete. This is assuming five years to build the infrastructure of the networked economy in the test nation, followed by three years of testing. The first year of tests will inevitably find flaws in the programming and the rules that businesses chose to compete under. The second year will be spent adjusting the flaws in the system and the third year will be another test. By the time the testing is complete in the test nation, the rest of the world will probably have most of their infrastructure in place. Assuming that is true, three years of testing for them would enable us to make the total transition from a money economy to a networked economy in eleven years. If we really got on the ball, we could make December 31, 2024 the day the money economy dies and we create a stable, efficient, competitive economy.

Overcoming the Obstacles to Networked Capitalism

Social Obstacles. There are four social obstacles in the way, preventing us from moving toward a networked economy. By social obstacles, I mean that there are beliefs that many people hold dear, which will stop them from accepting a new economic system. The great thing about social obstacles is that they exist only as long as we agree that they exist. All we have to do is decide that they aren't important anymore and they are gone. The bad thing is that they exist because people like them, and they will have trouble giving them up.

The first social obstacle is that money has become no less than the God of the modern capitalist economy.[18] Often when I talk to people about no longer using money, I get a look as if I am suggesting throwing one of their children off a cliff. People love money. We all dream of making millions, maybe billions, of whatever currency our nation uses. We all dream of giving our loved ones secure, prosperous lives.

Our society treats wealthy people like royalty, and secretly if not openly we all would like to be in that group.[19] Many people have asked me, "What would people strive for if there wasn't money? What will be their reward?" They believe money is their goal, when their real goal is all of the things they think money buys: Not only cool gadgets and an opulent lifestyle but also happiness, health, security, a long and fulfilling life, and a happy and healthy family. Many people mix up their desire for money with their desire for what money can provide them in our current economy.

We will all have the economic resources to help us find every one of these goals after we transition to a networked economy. The key to overcoming this obstacle is getting this fact through to the people who refuse to believe it. Using a limited money commodity to exchange goods and services actually hinders us, even in affluent nations, from building a truly safe, secure, and affluent nation and world. We will have to kill this false god, money, before we can move on to a life where everyone has these things without money.

The second social obstacle that lives deep in the minds of many people is the cynicism toward alternatives to the current capitalist

---

[18] See Wiseman, 1974, and Simmel, 1907, p. 27.

[19] Dodd, 1994, p. 154; Weber, 1956, p. 203; Simmel, 1907, pp. 238, 162; see also Gansmann, 1988, p. 292.

system, or even just criticism of the capitalist economy. The Cold War convinced us that there are only two kinds of economies: capitalist and communist. Cold War propaganda taught us that any criticism of one must be a promotion of the other. In reality, though, people throughout history have come up with many ways to run their economies.[20]

Nomadic tribes, for example, make decisions about who goes out hunting for animals, who gathers fruits from local plants, and who plants crops to be harvested later. When those people come back with their plants and dead animals for food, the tribe decides how to distribute the food to the various tribal families. Other people in the tribe, or maybe the same people at different times, make things like clothes, shoes, and weapons. The tribe has other customs that govern how these good are distributed.

Other small tribal societies have gift economies, where a person's prestige is based on how much they can give away to their neighbors. They have ceremonies where everyone comes to eat and the host family gives away as many of their possessions as they can. Then, later, their neighbors have their own ceremonies and give their possessions away to their neighbors, including back to the first family. Every family in the tribe takes their turn giving things to everyone else. That way goods circulate throughout the community and everyone has what they need, not through acquisition but through giving.

A few nations tried to take the economy of the small commune and stretch it to a large economy. It did not work. The wise community elders of the commune who make the planting decisions to everyone's best interests turned into the dictatorial bureaucracy of a communist state. Communism is dead as a system for running large, complex economies. It does not work. The central committee will make decisions in everyone's best interest only when they know everyone, like they do in a small commune. It is human nature. We care most for the people we know. That is the fatal flaw in trying to make a national communist economy.

Capitalism works much better. We all make the decisions that are best for ourselves and the economy adapts to our needs based on all of

---

[20] Polanyi named three ways communities have used throughout history to organize their economies: reciprocity as in tribal economies and gift economies, redistribution as in communism, and exchange as in mercantilism and capitalism. Polanyi, 1992, pp. 32-3.

those little decisions. However, it is not perfect as we have discussed. The economy is horribly volatile, very few people have enough money to do what they need to do, and great ideas, like trying to fuel our automobiles without polluting our atmosphere, fail because they cannot fit inside of the budget constraint. Then those ideas become viable only when other fuels become more expensive.

Human beings have spent their whole history trying different ways to run their economies. The current system arrived in the past century and a half with the winds of change and technological advancements. More advancement will lead us to the next innovation, and the next system. That system will exist until someone comes up with an even better idea. And so on, and so on, forever. Change is the only constant in life and in history. Networked capitalism is an improvement upon capitalism, not a turn toward communism.

The third social obstacle is that money enables us to believe in the conceit that wealth and prestige should lead to a better lifestyle. We believe that higher paying jobs are more valuable to society and therefore the people who occupy those jobs deserve their more lavish lifestyle. The poor, on the other hand are assumed to be lazy, ignorant, criminal, etc.[21]

We will have to get over this conceit. When we adopted democracy, we had to get over the idea that only those with royal titles had the right to their own religion, to speak their minds, to choose their friends, to justice under the law, *etc.*[22] Those without royal title had to worship the king's God, agree to his ideas, not join opposition groups against the king, and were lucky if they received just punishments. When we adopt a system for economic equality, we will have to learn that we all have a right to economic life, liberty, and happiness.

The fourth social obstacle to implementing networked capitalism will be the idea that there are several industries built around the study and management of money and those industries will be gone. They will be obsolete in a networked economy, just like the guild system

---

[21] See Bauman, 1998, pp. 63-80; See also Klebanow and Lowenkopf, 1994, for more on money, poverty, and the psychological consequences thereof.

[22] This didn't happen over night of course. In fact our American ancestors created the upper house of the United States legislature, the Senate, as a body initially appointed by state legislatures and not elected directly by the people because the founding fathers did not fully trust democracy. Even at the founding of the United States, poor people could not vote. Only land owning, white men could vote. Everyone else had to accept their opinions and views on policy and the proper direction of the country.

became obsolete when we moved to an industrial system for manufacturing goods. We will talk more about what those industries are in the section on what a networked economy will look like, but my earlier research estimated that about eight percent of the workforce will lose their current jobs when we switch to a moneyless economy. It will not be a sudden loss for many of them as implementation will take a more than a decade, but it will happen. Those people will have to explore their other talents and find jobs in other industries.

It will not be easy for the people losing their jobs, certainly, but the inconvenience will be for a good cause. In the end, their children and their children's children will be better off in the networked economy. Plus, the people losing their jobs will not be hurt economically by the change, since their lives will be better afterwards. They will just have to find other jobs. The good news is that other industries will be strengthened by the transition to a networked economy. Demand for goods and services will increase dramatically, which means that all types of manufacturing industries will boom. Also, think of all of those entertaining and exciting things we would like to do if only we could afford to do them. Those fun forms of recreation will all be possible for everyone in a networked economy and the industries surrounding those activities will be busier.

Political Obstacle. The political obstacle to transitioning to a networked economy is fewer in number but even more daunting. The political obstacle is the fact that few nations could adopt a networked economy on their own. A networked economy is a system that only works when the network can produce everything that the population in that network needs, including oil, timber, cars, clothes, food, etc. Everything. Few nations can produce everything their people need in this complicated world. Plus, there are some nations that would create economic devastation in the rest of the world if they were the only nation to remove themselves from the global money economy.

If this idea catches on in some parts of the world but not in others, it is possible for a group of nations who can produce everything that their citizens need to take themselves off of the money economy grid and create a networked economy among themselves while the rest of the world maintains a money economy. The two types of economies could not trade, however, because the money economy would demand a medium of exchange that the networked economy does not have.

It would be best if we all make the transition together. That means global education and global political negotiation. If this idea takes off, I am going to be traveling and traveling, and traveling. All of the nations of the world will participate in the debate and every nation will need to move together to implement the networked economy. If there is anything I have learned talking to people about these ideas, it is that the ideas stimulate questions. Many, many questions arise, which is why I have included the "Common Comment" in this text to help us explore those questions. Hopefully we can answer enough questions to convince everyone that we would all be better off in a networked economy.

Technological Obstacle. We do not need advanced technology to manage a networked economy. The simplest computers with the slowest internet connections could transmit the simple data needed to calculate supply and demand and get the 'approved' or 'rejected' response from the bank computers about whether a person is employed or not. The problem is access to the internet and the existence of high-speed transmissions lines. According to the website Internet World Stats[23], only 25 percent of people around the globe have access to the internet. That varies by region from 74 percent in North America to 7 percent in Africa. In Africa, it varies by country from zero percent to almost 13 percent in Egypt. Since the last time I looked at this data, around the year 2000, until 2009, internet access has grown almost 400 percent. At that rate, happily, everyone who needs access will have it by the time we get around to implementing this economy.

The good news is that every individual will not necessarily need to have internet access to make the economy work. Every business, however, will need to be linked to the internet. Plus, we should remember that there are some areas that are not really part of the global economy. Certain traditional areas mostly take care of themselves and only tangentially have contact with the global economy. They will not need to be wired to the internet and the economic network. These areas include the Amish communities and farming communes in the United States, Canada and Europe, some small islands in the South Pacific, tribal areas of Africa and Asia, and other places around the world where people support themselves without needing to trade with the outside world.

Once we get over these obstacles: coming to terms with the reality that everyone will be economically equal, getting the whole world on board with this transition, and creating the technological

---

[23] http://www.internetworldstats.com/stats.htm

infrastructure to manage the networked economy, we can move on to implementing networked capitalism. The networked economy, in the simplest terms, is just an accounting system with a different set of rules, so it can be set up and run along side of the money commodity for as long as we need to test it.

Setting up Networked Capitalism in a Test Nation

Before we set up a networked economy across the globe, though, we should set it up and test it for a few years in a small country. The other nations of the world can provide this nation with all of the goods and services it needs while it tests the networked economy. The ideal test nation will be a small island nation with an affluent population and a stable government. A small nation would not hurt the global economy if it went offline, and an island will stop cross-border contamination of the test from people smuggling out free goods to sell on the money-driven market. Tourism will be cut off for the few years while the economy is being tested, and exports will be banned. Only residents will be able to come and go from the test nation.

An example of an ideal test nation would be Iceland, which has a small, well-educate population and one of the oldest stable governments on the planet. Apologies to the people of the great nation of Iceland for just throwing their name out there, but they really are a very good choice. Their government was established over a thousand years ago, they are geographically isolated to prevent test contamination, and their 300,000 person population is 92 percent urban, 99 percent literate, and 100 percent democratic.

Whatever nation is used for the test, they will be the launching pad into a new era of human existence. With that said, onward we go to the implementation of the networked economy. The first three steps of the implementation process can happen at the same time.

Step 1: Determine Sustainable Demand

The sum total of human demands, every good or service that we would or could want or need is infinite. All of the wants and needs that occur to our little minds all day and night have no end, from the "Gee wouldn't that be nice to have!" to the "We have to get that!" and the "Oh no! I have to pay for THAT?" The whole list of all these needs and wants is the "absolute demand" for each of us. It is what we would buy if we had the economic power to buy everything that we need and want on a daily basis.

If we wanted to figure out how much the whole society wants, we could add up the absolute demand for each person, and then we could add up the various nations around the world to figure out the global absolute demand. No economy could ever meet every demand that every person can think of, and we should not even try. It probably would not be healthy for us to have everything we can think of anyway, even if it were possible.

Adam Smith was the first to talk about "expressed demand", which is the fraction of the absolute demand that can be expressed because we have the money to make it happen.[24] Supply and demand do not actually interact with each other; they both interact with money. People can only express as much of their demand as their budget will allow. Here is that diagram again.

Supply and Demand Filtered Through the Money Supply

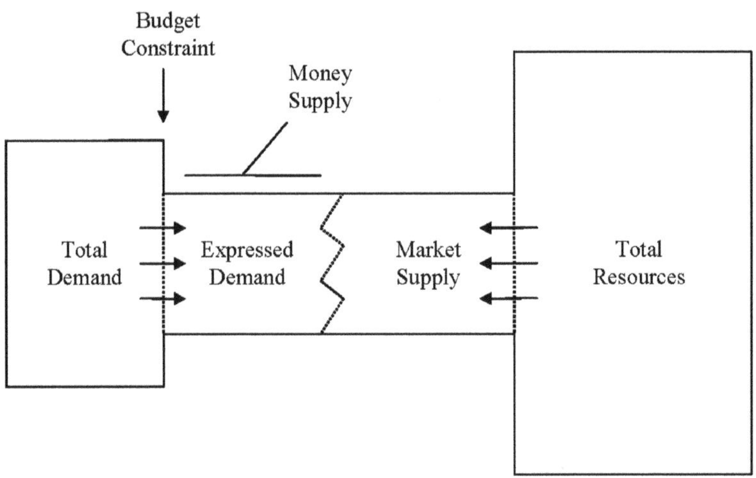

Supply and demand only meet if there is enough money floating through the economy to allow consumers to express the demand.

[24] Smith, 1776, pp. 158-9. This distinction is carried forth throughout the economic and sociological literature. See also Helferrich, 1927, p. 280; Veblen, 1904, pp. 216-7; Keyes, 1979, pp. 82, 89; Weber, 1956, p. 108; Simmel, 1907, p. 92.

Somewhere between the amount of demand that the money economy allows us to express and the infinite number of human desires that we have is what the environment can sustainably support. That is the sustainable demand of the planet. Before we can make the transition to a networked economy, we need to figure out our planet's sustainable level of production. How much of our resources can we withdraw from the environment every year to meet the needs of the population without ever running out of global resources?

A networked economy will bring us face to face with the challenge of creating enough goods and services to satisfy every person on the planet, without consuming ourselves out of a planet. We live in a world of scarce resources and if the whole world consumed as much and as wastefully as many people do now, we would need several planets to satisfy everyone.

We need to do research to determine how much people would consume if they can consume anything. I can think of two ways to answer this question. First, we could look at the consumption habits of very wealthy people. They are notoriously shy about participating in research, but perhaps they will open up for the sake of the future of the planet. We might be surprised at what we find. If books like *The Millionaire Next Door*[25] are any indication, people who really can consume anything, do not really consume that much. It is people like lawyers and financial advisers, who service these very wealthy people who are the real consumption hogs, because they are trying to look wealthier than they are.

The second way that we can find out what people would consume if they could consume anything is to ask them in surveys and panels, and ask them to keep diaries that keep track of what they want but cannot buy for lack of money. All of these methods are frequent and common in social science research.

Finally, we need to determine if we can produce enough goods and services to satisfy people enough so that they support the new economy. If we cannot produce enough with our current capacity, we can create policies to bring our production closer to the required consumption either by improving production capabilities or decreasing required production. As the transition is taking place, governments of the world should get together to increase productive capacity around the world as much as possible. For example, we should maximize the

---

[25] Stanley, 1998.

ability to produce food by building desalination plants around the world to provide potable water and irrigate as much as land as possible. The surface of our planet is seventy-five percent water. It is about time we take full advantage of that fact.

There are also several ways that we might decrease the required production and make it easier to meet as many needs as possible. First, we can start by increasing the amount of recyclable and recycled materials that we use in our goods and services closer to 100 percent. The more we reuse and reuse our resources, the less we have to take new resources out of the environment. We can develop practices that use the same tools over and over again. We can use and reuse more recyclable synthetic materials, like some plastics, in manufacturing goods. Then, when those goods are no longer useful, we can recycle the materials to make other goods in the future.

Second, we can develop product designs that make it easier to disassemble products after they are used. If a mobile phone for example was made with a recyclable case and well organized components, the used phone could be easily taken apart and the components would be easily separated and put back in the manufacturing system to make new products. If we think about the need to reuse materials from the beginning of the manufacturing process, it will make recycling much easier and enable us to more efficiently use limited resources to meet more and more human need.

Third, we can increase the useful life of our goods and services by using sturdier construction and better-made materials. Products can be designed with high quality materials to last a long time, or they can be designed with minimally acceptable materials to minimally acceptable standards to last a while and then break so that the customer needs to buy a new product. Repeat customers are the key to a business' success in a money economy after all. However, if we want to get the most out of our economy with limited resources we can require that products be made to last as long as possible. Because the networked economy will not have to worry about profit from repeat customers, businesses will not be hurt if every business is required to make long lasting products. Businesses will compete to serve the level of demand that exists, whatever level of demand that is.

Fourth, we can change our waste management system from a "Bury and Forget" system into a "Product Disassembly and Material Reclamation" system. What are now garbage dumps will in a networked economy take apart our used goods and separate out the precious metals and recyclable materials. This will create a new industry to make our recycling more efficient. Then, we can stop relying on people to remember to recycle their trash. The waste industry will automatically recycle as much as can be recycled.

Fifth, we can move away from using materials that cannot be recycled. We can actively look for ways to replace non-recyclable materials with recyclable materials in our product designs. As products evolve and upgrade, engineers can be on the look out for ways to use less and less from the environment and make our production system more and more sustainable. Researchers can also actively develop new sturdy, recyclable synthetic materials that can be used for making products, buildings, vehicles, *etc.* and then after they have lived their useful life, the materials can be broken down and reused in future products, buildings, vehicles, *etc.*

Eventually, we may get back to a point where nature is producing many more resources than we are using. The forests will be full of trees, the oceans will be teeming with fish, and the underground aquifers will be full of rain water because we use recyclable synthetics for building things, manage the fisheries effectively, and desalinate ocean water to irrigate our fields and meet our water needs.

In reality, though, we will not know how much people will consume until we actually make the transition to a networked economy, because there are cultural issues surrounding money and buying things. Today, we might think that people will buy tons of things because today there is prestige in being able to buy tons of things. In a society where anyone can buy anything, though, there will be nothing special about the person who owns the hot new thing. The cultural beliefs will change. At first, consumption might be very high, but then that might change if people start seeing high consumption as wasting valuable resources. That might evolve to be considered rude and consumption might decline. We do not know.

All we can do is make our best guess about how much people will consume, educate people about what is going to happen, do our best to produce enough goods and services so that people will accept the new system, and then be ready to adapt to the changing realities when we actually make the transition to a networked economy and the inevitable surprises pop up.

One thing we have also seen in areas where some resource falls below what we need, like the water shortages in California for example, is that people are very flexible in their consumption. If the population is asked to slow down their consumption of a particular good or service while production catches up to demand, they are very understanding and compliant about following that request. This gives me great hope in our ability to develop a system where we manage the global resources to meet the needs of every person on the planet.

Step 2: Software Program to Manage the Economic System

We will need a simple software package that will enable competition measurement offices to collect sales data from businesses on a daily basis. The program should be something that merchants can load on their computers and use to log onto their accounts with their CMO. The best program will be a simple, numbers-oriented program that can be plugged into any website, so that the same program can be used in any language, for any country.

The banking system will need a separate network to verify consumer employment similar to the credit card purchasing system in place now to manage the communication between merchants around the world and banks around the world. They can just adapt the credit card network for their purposes, since credit will be an obsolete concept without money.

Step 3: Create Bank/Competition Measurement Office Network

The federal and state governments will have to create competition measurement offices ("CMOs") within their tax collection agencies. If people object to this function being housed within the government, the legislatures can create independent public entities to serve this function. Either way, once the offices are created, businesses around the world will have to coordinate with their competitors to develop their rules of competition and communicate those rules with their CMOs.

Banks will need to include employment information in their account records, and the banking system as a whole will need to adapt the credit card readers that are all over the world to link in with their systems to verify employment. Banks will also have to include information on who a person's dependents are, since the dependents will also need to acquire goods and services based on the consumer's employment.

Step 4: Issue Bank Cards to the Population

After the Bank/CMO networks are in place, the banks will need to issue bank cards to consumers and teach their customers how to use the cards. This step is not going to be hard. Life in a networked economy will be like putting everything we need on a credit card with no limit and then never paying the bill. People get used to that concept pretty fast from what I have seen. Remember that membership in the new economy is based on employment and that dependents' membership is based on their affiliation with the consumer. So, the dependents will have to be issued their own bank cards from the consumer's account.

Using a bank card will be like using a debit card. People will go to a store, choose their items from the shelves, and take their items to the counter. The clerk will scan the items and the consumer will swipe their card through a reader. Then the consumer will have to enter a personal identification number into the machine. The machine will send the information to the bank, the bank will respond with an "approved" or "rejected", and the consumer will either take their goods from the store, if the transition is approved, or they will not, if the transaction is rejected.

Education of the population is the most important part of this process, because the foundation for the success of any economy is the trust that the population holds for the economy.[26] If the population does not trust an economic system, they will not use it. They will develop an underground economy and take care of their needs that way. That is why the implementation process should be very, very slow. It should be excruciatingly slow, really, so that people are very aware of what is happening and what is going to happen. They should get to a point where they are clamoring for the next stage to come.

Step 5: Rewrite the Criminal Code of Laws

The punishment for violating most minor laws is a money fine. For example, we have to pay some small amount of money for violating the speed limit while we are driving and automobile. The criminal legal code includes language for each violation, providing details that the punishment is up to a certain amount of money and a

[26] Goodhart, 1989, pp. 33-4; See also Simmel, 1907, pp. 125, 142, 178-9, 242; Dodd, 1994, pp. 136-43.

certain amount of time in jail. All of those laws will have to be rewritten to set up non-monetary punishments for those crimes. Different legislatures will come at the task from different directions. Perhaps, the resolution will be counseling on whatever the violation is, perhaps public service, perhaps something indirectly related to the offense, like spending a few hours picking up trash near the place a person was caught speeding in their automobiles. However they resolve it, we cannot impose fines in an economy without money, so our governments will have to find other ways to punish people who break minor laws.

Step 6: Test the Networked Economy Along Side of the Money Economy

The networked economy is basically an alternative accounting system, so it can be set up and run along side of the money economy without disrupting the money economy. Once the bank and CMO networks are in place, businesses have created their rules of competition, and everyone has been issued their bank cards, people can start using the networked economy. Naturally, they will only be able to acquire what they can pay for, since the money economy will still be in effect. But, when we buy things we will pay money and we will also swipe our bank cards to show our employment. Perhaps if we use a credit card for the purchase, the credit card networks can be reprogrammed to do both the money transaction and the networked transaction automatically. Some governments may mandate credit card use for every purchase in order to make testing more efficient.

We can test this system for at least two years, to measure how demand changes seasonally for each industry in each market. We can determine if the rules that the competitors chose were appropriate for their market. We can also make sure that communication is fluid around the world between merchants, banks, and competition measurement offices. Any new system has bugs to be worked out and this new system will be no exception. Naturally, we have no idea what the problems with the new system will be right now. Testing the new system for at least two or three years will enable us to address these glitches, make the needed changes to the system, retest the system and measure performance over all four seasons, and give us time to fine tune the needed adjustments to the system.

Step 7: Increase Production to Meet Anticipated Demand

Once the testing is complete and we are satisfied that the system will work the way we want it to work, producers will increase their production and fill their warehouses in anticipation of the new level of demand that the economy will need to handle.

Step 8: Discontinue the Money Economy

When all of the previous steps are completed, the production has been ramped up to meet the expected demand, and every person in the world knows what is going to happen, perhaps on some December 31st in the next few decades, we will stop using money and just use the bank cards to acquire the goods and services that we need.

Hopefully the day after we stop using money will be a lot like the day before we stop using money. People will be secure in their knowledge that the economy will go on successfully and they will not rush to the stores. They will treat the new economy like the infant that it will be and be gentle, increasing their demand slowly. Of course people who have real needs will meet those needs, but those with mere wants will hold off on satisfying those until later. They will give the new economy three months, six months, maybe a year to take its baby steps. Those of us with plenty in our lives might even scale back our consumption a little and let those who live without enough goods and services to step forward. Then, over time, as the networked economy works itself into a rhythm and people develop their new patterns of consumption, the system will be able to stretch its legs and we can move into the future as a prosperous people.

It will take some time before the network is truly diversified in every corner of the globe. The networked economy will be set up along side of the money economy, which means that the goods and services that are available in the networked economy right after the transition will be the same ones that were available in the money economy just before the transition. In truly undeveloped economies, many types of goods and services are absent from their markets. It will take time for those businesses to be created. Local governments might help potential local business owner operators find these businesses and get set up serving the local community.

* * *

So, there it is: the transition from money capitalism to capitalism without money. We set up the infrastructure, write the rules of competition, educate everyone how to use the new system, set up the new system in tandem with the old system, test the new system until it is ready to go, and then discontinue the old system. If we first set up the networked economy in a small test nation, we should be able to complete the process within five years. Then we can test it in that nation for a few years. If it looks good to go, we can create the infrastructure around the world. That should only take a few years since they will probably start developing their infrastructure before we are done testing the networked economy in the test nation. Then, if we test the global system for three years before we stop using money, we will have a total transition time of fourteen years.

So what will it be like living in a society that does not use money? What will the economy look like after we stop using money? How will our lives be different? How will society change? The next chapter discusses what a networked society will look like.

Chapter 5

Living in a Networked Economy

As was mentioned in a previous chapter, living in a networked economy will be like using a no-limit credit card to pay for everything and then never paying the bill. What affluent people do on a daily basis will not be very different when we switch over, and we will all have many more options in a networked economy. Think of all of those things we would like to do, if only we could afford it. In an economy free to produce enough for everyone, we will all be able to do whatever we like doing. Everyone else in the world will be able to do them as well. So, there will no longer be poverty, there will be less crime, and more prosperity around the world. The economy will also be more resilient against sudden catastrophes whether they are natural or manmade.

Common Comment: Sounds like some silly fantasy of a perfect world. You don't really believe that's possible.

Not a Perfect World

A perfect world? Absolutely not. And this will not be a perfect world. This book is about better managing our economy to make it more stable, productive and efficient, and making our material lives easier. We will not have to worry anymore about making enough money to pay for everything we need today and saving money for everything we will need in the future. Networked capitalism will make the economy stable by taking away the limited money commodity and its wild fluctuations. Along with money, we will get rid of the boom and bust business cycle and the recessions and depressions that cause so much suffering. We will also make the economy more productive and efficient by taking away the budget constraint and by using the full resources of the environment to meet the demands of the whole population instead of just the people who have money. We will also be able to use the labor and creativity of people who now live in places with undeveloped money economies. All of our lives will be a lot "richer" in networked economy.

There is more to life than buying things and eating food, however. There is family and love, for example. This economy will not make the more challenging members of our families any easier to deal with, although we will not have money issues to fight over.[27] Convincing our children to study before dinner and to eat their vegetables will not be any easier. Although parents will not have to worry about paying for the constant stream of expenses that come with raising a child like clothes, summer camp, clothes, braces for crooked teeth, clothes, that first car, college, and of course clothes, clothes, and clothes.

For the unmarried among us, the new economy will not make it any easier to talk to that girl, or get the attention of that guy, although we will be able to spend more time "out and about" looking for that special someone, and we will have the ability to do more interesting things while we are looking for that special someone. In as much as being wealthy and being able to provide a secure home makes a guy more confident in talking to the ladies, though, the networked economy will help with that. Although, she will not need his economic support to make her secure, so he better be nice.

There are also health issues to think about. Creating a networked economy will not automatically find us a cure for cancer, diabetes, AIDS, the H1N1 flu, or any of the other diseases ravaging the human race. Other viruses, bacteria, fungi, and diseases around the world will also continue to evolve, looking for new and better ways to infect us so that they may survive and thrive. The networked economy will help us research ways to fight them, however, since researchers will be able to work on whatever they want to spend their time doing, without the endless search for grant money. The networked economy will also help get rid of the illnesses associated with hunger, since we will have the resources to finally feed every person on the planet.

Networked capitalism will not suddenly make our lives easy and effortless. We will all still have to work and contribute to our

---

[27] Financial issues are the number one contributor to relationship tension and divorce. See Rubenstein, 1980; Argyle and Henderson, 1985; Poduska and Allred, 1990; Doyle, 1992b; Klebanow and Lowenkopf, 1994; Singh, 1996; Dalphonse, 2000.

economy. This will not be some Garden of Eden where we lay around all day eating grapes and melons. We will still have to exercise to stay healthy. If we eat too much and exercise too little, we will still get fat and give ourselves heart disease, no matter how we organize the economy.

Creating a networked economy will not do anything to help with political issues. Should gay men and lesbian women be able to marry? Should we legalize the possession or use of any drugs that are currently illegal? Should we criminalize aborting a pregnancy? How about burning a flag in protest? Should we use the death penalty for heinous crimes? How much should a government voice support for any one religion? How much religion should there be in our government policies? Is genetic research ethical? How about embryonic stem cell research? Should people suffering through a painful, terminal illness be able to end their own lives? Political issues will continue to drive our vigorous debates in a moneyless economy.

Social issues will also still be around in a moneyless economy. We will still have racism and sexism, and neo-Nazi fascism and all of the other hate-based "–isms" out there. Addictions of all kinds will still haunt some of us. We will still argue over public education. What should we teach our children in the public schools? Should we teach them about evolution? How should our school books address events in our past that we are not proud of, like slavery or the internment of Japanese-American citizens during World War II? Should we teach teenagers about sex and/or family planning? There are always issues of public "decency": How much skin should people be able to show in public? Is there too much sex and violence in movies, video games, and television? There are plenty of social issues for us to argue about.

We will still have crime. Money is a huge motivation for committing crime and a networked economy will get rid of a certain amount of crime; however some people will still lose their tempers and assault other people, sometimes even kill them. Some people will drink too much alcohol and decide to get behind the wheel of a car, causing accidents. Unfortunately, there will still be the physical, sexual, and emotional abuse of children. If I think of a way to get rid of that, I will definitely let you know. We will talk more about how crime will change shortly.

There is no such thing as a utopia. The reason for that is because people are imperfect. No matter how we organize our society, we can never make it perfect, because we are human. However, our goal is not to create a perfect society. Our goal is the same as the goal for the person who first suggested leaving the cave and living in manmade homes instead. It is the same goal as the person who suggested following the herds of wild animals, so we can kill them and eat them all year long. The same as the person who first suggested planting crops and herding animals to give us stable communities so that we did not have to move around all the time. It is the same as the person who suggested building a sewer system to get rid of all of that disease-causing garbage and human waste in the streets. It is the same as the person who suggested that we organize fire departments to protect everyone's homes, instead of one house catching fire and the whole city burning down. Every time a new technology or a new way of organizing our lives comes along, people use it to improve our situation and our communities.

The goal in writing this book is to make a better society and a better world. The Preamble to the United States Constitution lists six reasons why the founders created this great nation: to 1. Form a more perfect union, 2. Establish justice, 3. Insure domestic tranquility, 4. Provide for the common defense, 5. Promote the general welfare, and 6. Secure the blessings of liberty to ourselves and our posterity. That is my goal in writing this book, not only for the United States but for the whole world.

The divisiveness and instability that surrounds using a limited money medium of exchange, and the inequality that comes with it, creates imperfections in our union, undermines justice, disrupts domestic tranquility, increases the number of people we need to defend our nation against, diminishes the general welfare, and makes liberty more tenuous for ourselves and our children's children. A networked economy will make our society and our world more perfect, just, tranquil, secure, prosperous, and free.

The Negative Consequences of Networked Capitalism

There are, however, a few ways that a networked economy will make the world more complicated. The first is that it will make us more dangerous to this planet and make recycling an absolute necessity.

This effect has already been noted, but it bears repeating for emphasis. For those of us who would rather not be bothered to think about where their garbage goes once they toss it out, this is not good news. If we take off the reigns of the budget constraint and enable producers to take as much oil, wood, minerals, fish, and heavy metals from the environment that they can in a 24 hour manufacturing workday, and then just throw all of those materials away after we use them, we would soon be out of raw materials. There are almost seven billion people on this planet, and we are projected to be nine billion people by the year 2050.

If we are going to manage this economy so that everyone gets what they need, we will have to change our philosophy about how we design products. We will need to design them keeping in mind what we will do with them after we are done as I wrote about in more detail above. We will use more recyclable materials so that products can be broken down and their components can be reused. Electronic products will be designed so that new software features can be added in later without buying an entirely new product. All of our products will be designed to be long lasting, and then enable easy disassembly after we are done with them.

A second way that a networked economy will make life more complicated is that it will make participating in our government and keeping it transparent even more important.[28] We will all need to add our voices to public debate and keep an eye on what the government is using its large administrative abilities to do. Why? The government will not have a budget constraint either and it will be able to do whatever it decides to muster the resources to do.

That will be good on the one hand because there will be no more epic budget battles and fighting over whether we should cut or increase funding for education, benefits to the poor, the military, or fixing bridges and building the infrastructure. We will be able to do all of those things. The states and local governments will be able to maintain the infrastructure of roads, highways, bridges, water treatment plants, electric generation and transmission, *etc.* without interference from the federal government.

The federal government, meanwhile, will be able to build an efficient, disciplined, principled federal police force and military, and that is why keeping the federal government transparent will become even more important than it is today. For those of us who like to keep government power to a minimum, keeping an eye on the government will become very important. Unwatched governments have a history of

---

[28] See Bellah et al., 1992.

doing some very nasty things in the past, like conducting experiments on unsuspecting citizens without telling them. Either way, we will not be able to afford to leave the government alone to do whatever it wishes. Fortunately, there are networks of watchdog groups who find that kind of work very energizing.

The third way that networked capitalism will make the world more complicated is related to the second way. Networked capitalism is designed to be a global economy. That means that our government will be able to function without budget worries, and so will every other government in the world. That is good for the citizens of developing nations because their economies will be able to develop easier. They will no longer have to stretch anemic budgets to build an economy, or drown in debt trying to leverage scant funding to build roads and farms to feed their people. It is bad for the citizens of oppressive regimes because those regimes will be able to oppress their citizens easier. It will also be easier for these regimes to provide food and shelter for their people and keep their population satisfied. This will complicate things for those people who want to democratize these regimes. People who are well fed do not usually take to the streets.

Those are the negative effects of a networked economy. We will be forced to increase the quality and lifespan of the goods that we produce, and design them to be upgradable and recyclable. We will have to keep a closer watch on democratic governments and we will have a harder time convincing nondemocratic nations to become democratic. There are many more positive effects that a networked economy will have on our lives. I will discuss seven positive changes that the networked economy will bring to our lives.

No Money Worries

The most profound difference in our daily lives between living in a money economy and living in a networked economy will be that we will not have to worry about money anymore. We will no longer have to argue about money, and an accident or a poor life choice, like teen pregnancy, will no longer have the power to send us into lives of poverty and misery. We will be able to get our children everything they need to grow up happy and healthy, including those braces for their teeth, clothing, education, and a well rounded upbringing. We will be able to send them off to college, and then plan crazy vacations when the nest is empty. We will be able to enjoy our lives today without constantly worrying whether we will have enough money to retire with tomorrow. When we get there, we will be able to retire without constantly worrying that we might run out of money before we die. A crashing economy will not be able to yank us out of retirement after we have spent a lifetime saving diligently so that we can retire in peace. When we reach an age when our bodies do not do what we want them to do, and we need to be cared for all day and night, we will all be able to have the best care without burdening our families with the cost of expensive full-time healthcare.

We spend way too much time focusing on money: making money, spending money, making more money, saving money, making more money, investing money, keeping the money we have, arguing over how much money the government takes from us, and of course wondering “How do I make more money?” What will we think about when we no longer have to worry about money all the time? We will all really enjoy finding out. We will be free to think about and pay attention to what we like, who we love, and what we want for our futures knowing that we will all be able to afford them.

The Evolution of Greed

The most fundamental cultural difference between life in a networked economy compared to living in a money economy will be how we think about our possessions and how we think about each other in terms of our possessions. One amazing and sad thing that I discovered as I studied the role of money in society is the ability of money to turn everything into a number.[29] This couch is a $1000 couch, but that couch over there is a $10,000 couch. That baseball player is pretty good, he is a $10 million player, but that player over there is a $50 million player. My friend likes one guy but he has no money, so they cannot do anything, while another guy treats her terribly, but he is very wealthy. Money has the ability to destroy the depth in the meaning of things and people reducing them to their market value.

---

[29] Simmel called this a “tragedy of human concept formation” and it is a common observation in the literature about money in society. See Simmel, 1907, pp. 81, 121, 157, 257, 277-79; Schumpeter, 1942, pp. 123-4; Baker, 1987, p. 116; Weber, 1956, pp. 80-81; Weber, 1946, p. 331. See also Zelizer, 1994, p. 18 for a discussion of how social relations also change the meaning of different ‘kinds’ of money depending on what the money is used for.

Common Comment:	***You aren't going to get all fuzzy on us are you?***

You do not believe me? Did you ever loan a friend some money, enough money so that it was not easy for you to loan it away and enough so that it was not easy for them to pay it back?

Common Comment:	***Yeah! And he never did pay that back! Good for nothing bum, he was.***

That is why we should think twice before loaning money to friends. Before you loaned him the money, he was a good enough guy to be a friend. If we loan money to a friend and our friend cannot pay it back, it puts tension on the relationship. That tension grows and grows the longer it takes them to pay back the money. Eventually all we think about when we think about that friend is the money they owe us and if they never pay us back, eventually the friendship will end. Now he is a "good-for-nothing bum".

I even studied the affect of money on the most emotional relationship that exists: a sexual relationship. After selling sex for a while, many prostitutes lose the emotional value that they previously put on sex, even in their private lives. Their clients fantasize that prostitutes are sex-crazed nymphomaniacs but that could not be further from the truth. They often eventually lose interest in sex completely, their dating lives suffer and they often lose the ability to find real connections with the opposite sex.[30]

What is going to happen to our lives, our friends, and the way we think about the world when we no longer have money around to reduce everything to a number? What will happen to our mating habits when money is not an issue? A guy's earning power is a huge part of how they are valued as prospective mates. What will happen when every person has equal earning power? What will happen when a woman can be financially secure no matter what guy she marries? Will that be the end of the "trophy wife" phenomenon? When we can acquire anything, how much will we emotionally value any particular object? Will we acquire things that we want for deeper reasons and then value those things more deeply?

---

[30] McKeaganey, 1996, pp. 82-94.

As I studied different types of economies that have existed through time from the feudal economies, to the gift economies of tribal island communities, to the World War II prisoner of war camp economies that developed between the prisoners using wooden match sticks,[31] I discovered something remarkable. As a child of the 1980s, I had always thought that greed was universal: people always wanted to get as much stuff as they could, and more stuff was always better.[32] I always thought that the Amish communities must be miserable having so few material things in their lives. What I found, though, was that what people have always valued most was not the possession of things, but the high esteem of their friends and neighbors. People are social animals, and we all want the people around us to think well of us. It is still self-interested, because we want it to make ourselves feel good, but it was not what I expected.

In the gift economy, a person's friends and neighbors were more impressed with them the more they gave away. In a money economy, people are more impressed with us based on how many possessions we can afford to buy. The band Nickelback wrote a song I really liked a while ago called "Rockstar" and one of the lyrics says: "We all just wanna be big rock stars; live in hilltop mansions, driving fifteen cars." And honestly, I would love living in a hilltop mansion with fifteen cars to choose from. How will this change in a networked economy?

In an economy where anyone can own fifteen cars, though, how impressive will that really be? In a money economy, it is impressive because it sets a person apart. Not everyone can do it, so the person who can do it must be pretty special. In a networked economy though, it is just wasteful. It will be about as impressive as a person today who spends every penny they have on candy bars, but never eats them. Imagine if a person spent every extra bit of money buying candy bars, thousands of them, piled inside his home from floor to ceiling. That would be just sad.

We can go back to the restaurant metaphor that I used in the introduction, where the money economy is like an "a la carte" restaurant where you get only what you can afford and a networked economy will be like an "all-you-can-eat" restaurant, where you pay one price for access and then you can get whatever you want from the food buffet. Imagine being a very poor person who can barely afford

---

31 Radford, 1945.

32 See Veblen, 1899, pp. 97-8 regarding conspicuous consumption.

to sit down in the restaurant, much less order from the menu. When waiters in a normal restaurant go by with expensive dishes, the poor person might be envious of the patrons who can afford those dishes. In a buffet though, the person would see the person with the good food and say, "They have that up there? I'm getting me some." There is no envy when everyone can have it so there is no prestige attached to the possession.

Also, think of a person in a buffet who piles several plates high with food, eats some part of it and then leaves the rest to waste. First, it is important to note that people do not do that in an "all-you-can-eat" buffet. They take what they are going to eat and leave the rest for other people. We can see from looking at all-you-can-eat buffets and all-inclusive resorts that people who can have whatever they want do not stuff themselves. They take what they need and leave the rest.

However, assuming someone did waste several plates of food, how would the other patrons feel about that person? Would he have the same status as the wealthy person who buys a hundred sports cars and leaves them wasting away in a showroom where he can gaze at them while his servants polish the fenders? No. They would probably think he is a pig. This is what some people call conspicuous consumption and it has prestige in a money economy, but it almost certainly will not have prestige in a networked economy.

Of course, there is no way any person can predict how a culture will change over time, but it seems that we will become less materialistic in a networked economy. We will still be self-centered, because all life is primarily self-interested, as we can see from the survival instinct that we are all born with. Our own lives and well being and that of the people closest to us are of primary interest to us. That will not change. Perhaps, though, we will become interested in deeper self-fulfillment and seek out things that enrich our lives on other levels besides merely material.

Smaller Labor Force, Shorter Work Week, Longer Vacations

The labor force will look very different in a networked economy. Money is such a big part of our lives that we have several industries built around making money, winning money, managing money, investing money to make more money, and protecting us against the sudden loss of our money. Research into the labor market of the

United States showed that between six and eight percent of the labor force will have to find another job as we make the transition to a networked economy. Other industries that are built around making things and providing entertainment will grow dramatically when we can afford to acquire any product and enjoy any experience that the economy offers.

The following table shows what will happen to different industries when we transition to a networked economy. The left column of industries will be obsolete after the transition to a networked economy, and the right column of industries will be helped dramatically by the loss of a money economy. The middle column of industries that have to do with money but not as a main function will be diminished in a networked economy.

Effects of Networked Capitalism on the Labor Force

Industries Made Obsolete:	Industries Diminished:	Industries Strengthened:
Accounting	Advertising	Education
Banking	Economics	Fitness
Foundations and Charities	Legal Services	Manufacturing
Fundraising	Lobbying and PACs	Recreation
Gambling	Organized Crime	Research/Invention
Insurance		Services of all kinds
Investments		Travel and Tourism
Tax Collection and Redistribution		
Tax Law		

Industries Made Obsolete

Financial Services. Financial services include everything that a financial planner would coordinate: accounting, banking, insurance, and investments. In an economy without money, there will be no assets or liabilities for an accountant to keep track of, and no tax returns to be filed, or fines to be paid. We will not need banks to keep our money safe, although I suggested above a new mostly automated role for banks in a networked economy, which will require less labor to function. We will not need to go talk to a bank teller in a networked economy.

Insurance protects us against the possibility of a tragic event overwhelming our money supply or costing us more money than we should pay. It covers monetary loss and protects our families from falling into poverty and financial misery. We will not need insurance in an economy where everything is free, including car repairs, hospital visits, home repairs, etc. This is exceptionally good news for one industry in particular, the health care industry, which suffers in their relationship with the health insurance industry. Doctors, nurses, hospitals, and clinics will be greatly relieved to be able to practice medicine how they want to practice it and take care of their patients in the way that is best for the patient. That is much better than caring for the patient only so much as is best for the insurance companies' profit margins.

Investments will also be unnecessary, not only because there will not be any money around to invest, but also because starting a business will be free, so the managers of the business will not need to sell ownership in the company or issue corporate bonds to fund company operations.

Foundations and Charities. These organizations exist to serve that large group of people who are not being served by the money economy: the poor, the sick, the disabled. Foundations and charities provide a method for us to use our money to help people and causes that cannot make enough money from the profit-driven market system. For many groups, charities are their only method of meeting the basic human needs that the money economy fails to provide. They provide a lifeline to humanity for these groups.

In a networked economy, though, no person will be left out of our society's prosperity. The economy, however, will still run on self-interest: a person will work to have access to the economy and to do work they enjoy. A business will serve as many people as possible in order to maintain their market share, and to keep their business license. There will be no poverty because any job will ensure an affluent lifestyle, and the sick and disabled will have access to the economy without the need to work. Research into illnesses will forge ahead without worrying about finding money to pay for it. Hospitals and treatment centers will be able to offer the sick and disabled the best care without worrying about a budget. So, we will not need foundations and charities any more.

Fundraising and Gambling. I combine these two only because the reason they will be abolished in a networked economy is equally obvious. There is no reason to raise funds in an economy where there is no such thing as "funds" needed to pay for causes and campaigns. Likewise, we cannot play a game of chance in hopes of winning big cash rewards in an economy where there is no cash.

Of course the "gaming" industry could convert to real "gaming" where the games are played just for the fun of it. Few people go to a gambling city seriously expecting to win big anyway. We go for the spectacle, the shows, and to let loose from our everyday lives. Imagine how vibrant and raucous the "gambling" would be if every person who went to a casino was given 10,000 credits worth of chips and invited to win as much as they can with their game-playing skills, with no downside? The tables would be teeming with action. The casinos can invent other rewards for the big winners, like the nicest suites on the strip.

Tax Law, Tax Collection and Redistribution. We will no longer have to worry about taxes in a networked economy. We also will not have to hear the constant bickering among politicians about cutting spending here or raising taxes there. The size and scope of the government as a whole will be very different, and much smaller, in a networked economy. All of the departments in charge of collecting our taxes and redistributing them to different segments of the population will be abolished. At last count for the United States Government, there were almost fifty government departments, offices, councils, programs and funds that will be abolished with the money economy. Most notable among these are the Department of the Treasury, which includes the Internal Revenue Service, although this book suggests transitioning the Internal Revenue Service into a Competition Measurement Office. Also abolished will be the Federal Reserve offices, the Federal Deposit Insurance Corporation, the Social Security Administration, and all of the welfare programs. The financial regulation system will also be abolished, including the Securities and Exchange Commission and the Financial Industry Regulatory Authority. Aside from these whole offices, there will be all of those money-centered occupations within the other departments, the budget officers, the accountants, and the clerks that handle accounts payable, accounts receivable and the like. The government will have a much smaller role in our lives in a networked economy.

Those are the industries that will be obsolete in a networked economy. Other industries will be merely diminished by this economic innovation: networked capitalism.

Industries Diminished

Advertising. Do you ever wish you could watch an hour-long television program that was actually an hour long, and not forty-four minutes long with sixteen minutes of commercials? Do you wish you could pick up your favorite magazine and flip right to the articles without going through page after page, after page, of advertisements? Would you like to listen to commercial free radio without paying extra for it? Do you ever wish you could drive down the highway without being forced to look at billboards trying desperately to get your attention without distracting you too much from your driving? Do you hate political advertisements that scare you with half-truths, ominous music and cynical innuendo? If so, here is some good news.

In a networked economy, magazines, newspapers, and broadcasts over radio and television will compete for viewers and readers, not for advertising dollars. After we make the transition to a networked economy, magazines will compete with other magazines for market share without worrying about money. Their CMO will compare their sales and they will have to maintain a certain market share, just like every business. None of these media will have to sell advertising space to survive. They will only have to broadcast and print things that attract and interest their customers. That means that we will be able to peruse the internet, read magazines, listen to the radio, and watch television without having to tolerate advertisements.

That reality will make life interesting for the advertising industry. They are very creative people and I am sure they will find other ways to let us know all about their products. Direct marketing will still exist: direct postal mail, electronic mail, in-person advertising. Viral marketing on the internet is always entertaining for the truly creative video advertisements. There is always another way to let people know about products and services, and the advertising industry will certainly find it.

Also, we may say that advertisements annoy us, but we really want to know about what products are available on the market. We will probably seek them out. Consumer magazines will become even more popular. Online product reviews are already more important than advertising for savvy shoppers. Maybe some company will start competing advertising channels, with the funniest, most clever advertisements. Hmm … it would be interesting to put the commercials for competing brands side by side to see who has better advertising and who is stretching the truth more. That is a great idea, actually. Someone should market that idea to the television studios.

Economics. The study of how people and businesses use their scarce money commodity to buy what they need from the economy will be quite different in an economy without money. One would think economics would become obsolete in a networked economy, but as long as there is production, distribution, and consumption, there will be economists around to track and measure them. Their role will be diminished. We will not have Federal Reserve Bank chairmen around to elevate to the status of rock stars, or cast down to the status of pariahs for that matter, depending on if they are mainly right or wrong most recently.

In our discussion so far, we have raised plenty of issues of interest to economists. How much demand can our planet's resources sustainably satisfy? How might we stretch that productive capability? How do we measure productivity without money? How could we improve upon the measure that I suggested: measuring productivity through sales per labor hour? All of these issues can be taken up by economists and they can add to our body of knowledge in that way.

Legal Services. As long as there are laws, there will be lawyers. Sorry, Shakespeare.[33] All areas of law will change when we take money out of the system, however. There are many different types of lawyers, though, some focusing more on money issues than others. Here are notes on a few of those legal specialties:

1. Trial Lawyers: I have already discussed how there will be less litigation in a networked economy because without money, there is no way to hurt someone financially. That will affect trial lawyers and there will be fewer of them. There will be no more ambulance chasers.

2. Tax Lawyers: With no more taxes, there will be no more tax laws, and consequently there will be no more tax lawyers.

3. Affordable Housing Lawyers: There is a legal specialty in affordable housing that will no longer be needed when everyone can afford a home.

[33] William Shakespeare, *Henry VI*, Part 2, Act 4, Scene 11, "The first thing we do, let's kill all the lawyers."

4. Estate Attorneys: The role of estate attorneys will change when trusts are no longer needed to manage the distribution of money among a person's descendants.
5. *Pro Bono* Work: This is free legal advice that lawyers provide to poor clients. The good news for the lawyers and the clients alike is that everyone will be able to afford quality legal advice in a networked economy and there will no longer be different classes of clients. Every person will have the right and the ability to access quality legal advice when they need it.
6. Cheap, Sleazy Lawyers: Along those same lines, when everyone will be able to afford quality representation, the new economy will also raise the overall quality of the legal profession. People who can afford anything will demand higher quality service every time. The demand for poor quality, "budget" lawyers will fall and lawyers as a group will have to adapt by becoming more skilled in order to attract clients.

Lobbying and Political Action Committees (PACs). Politicians use political action committees to advocate for their pet issues, to raise money to support candidates they like, and to raise money to be used for future political campaigns. Obviously the fundraising functions will be absent in a networked economy, but those people who are politically active will still use these committees to hire staff to advocate for whatever issues they feel strongly about.

Lobbyists use their expertise on a particular issue, the power of their political contributions, and the voting power of their clients' membership to try to get legislators to change pending legislation in ways that are favorable to their clients. Their clients are corporations and interest groups from all sections of society. Lobbyists also raise money for the politicians who are favorable to their issues. They host fundraisers and invite their clients' members to come, donate money, and talk to the members of Congress and their staffs about the issues that are important to their group. That is where the problem lies with the influence of money in the modern American government.

This is how some lobbyists get a bill through Congress: the lawyers who work with the lobbyist write the proposed legislation and they shop it around to the various members of Congress who have been friendly to them, asking the members to sponsor the legislation and introduce the bill to Congress. If a member of Congress agrees to consider the bill, the lobbyist throws a fundraiser for the member where executives from that industry contribute tens of thousands of dollars, or more, to the member's campaign fund.

If the member then decides not to sponsor the bill, the lobbyist looks for another member to sponsor the legislation. When they find another member willing to consider the legislation, that member gets a fundraiser. When the member introduces the bill, they get another fundraiser. When the bill passes, the member gets another fundraiser. Does that sound like corruption? It is. Does it sound like they are buying the legislation with fundraisers? They are. Unfortunately, it is not illegal, although it should be.

When a bill is being debated in the legislature, whether or not they originated the legislation, the lobbyists also use their relationships with members to gain access to key staff members and aggressively press the staff to add provisions they like and remove provisions they do not like. Lobbyists hire former members of Congress who have greater access to the floors of the houses of Congress, and to existing members, so that the lobbying firm has even more influence on the process.

Here is the problem: The United States of America is supposed to be a representative democracy. The people we elect to represent us are supposed to be representing the people in their districts who voted for them, and ideally even the people who did not vote for them. They should be doing what is best for everyone in their districts and then for the nation as a whole. Instead, they are representing the interests of the people who pay for their campaigns. And the people who pay for their campaigns are largely interest groups from outside of their districts. Money is undermining our democracy.

This is understandable, actually; it is human nature. Every person alive is very interested in the opinion of the person who pays them, enables them to keep their job, and to feed their family. For most of us, it is a person who works nearby, who keeps track of the work we do, and who tells us when we are doing a good job. For politicians, though, it is the people who pay for their campaigns, and politicians need a lot of money.[34] Running for office is very expensive, and it is only getting more expensive as every campaign needs advertising on

[34] Box-Steffensmeier, 1996, pp. 352

expensive media like television. Plus, now corporations can spend unlimited amounts of money on political advertising, which politicians must also defend against.

Every campaign also inevitably degenerates into smear contests where each campaign spends obscene amounts of money buying advertising to make the other person look as bad as possible. These late campaign smear-fests are really just competitions to see who has more money and who can blanket the airwaves more effectively. Many campaigns are won or lost not by the abilities of a candidate to impress voters with their position, but by negative advertising's ability to make the voters dislike the other person more. Politicians are only human for paying more attention to the interest groups that pay for their campaigns and keep them employed.

That being said, politicians are not passive, innocent victims in this corruption of American democracy, either. Many Congressional members' political staffs actively solicit donations from lobbyists, and the pressure to donate is immense. In fact, some politicians get elected to safe seats, spend a couple of terms in Congress, and then leave to become lobbyists themselves, which makes it look like the goal all along was to become a wealthy lobbyist. American government is in a sad state right now, largely due to the affect that money has on the political process.

A networked economy will return our democracy to the voters. The new economy will finally take money out of politics and return lobbyists to their role as industry experts and membership representatives, offering technical advice and letting legislators know what issues are most important to the voters back home that belong to the lobbyist's interest group.

Campaigns will also be free to every candidate, which means that anyone will be able to run for office, not just the wealthy. Anyone within the district with an opinion and the ability to convince people to vote for them will be able to launch a campaign. That will make our public debates much more diverse and far more interesting. Advertising will be free as well, although as I wrote above, the state of advertising will be dramatically different. Without the ability to flood the airways with negative advertisements full of half truths and exaggerations, politicians will have to return to good, old fashioned retail politics where they actually have to speak to the voters in rallies and meet them one on one.

Organized Crime. When Americans think of organized crime, they often think of the Italian American Mafia and other domestic gangs, but there are gangs and syndicates all over the world who make money from bribery, blackmail, credit card fraud, money laundering, extortion, kidnapping, human trafficking, prostitution, bookmaking, loan sharking, identity theft, and other crimes. Most of these crimes are crimes with money and will be abolished with the transition to a networked economy, which will diminish organized crime around the world. In a networked economy, it will be impossible to gain economic power from illegal activities because the system will have control over who has access to the economic network. As we saw above, economic power comes from working for accredited businesses, which obviously will not include illegal businesses. Converting to a networked economy will completely undermine the economic base of all organized crime throughout the world.

Organized crime pops up when the society is weak, disorganized, or when a marginalized group of people cannot trust the system of government. This is yet another reason why it is important that people trust the new economy before we implement it. We must take our time to introduce the new economy to the population and get them used to using it. This will happen mostly in the phase of the implementation where we are testing the network and people are using both the money economy and the networked economy.

These are the industries that will be diminished when we make the transition to a money economy: advertising, economic, illegal drugs, legal services, political lobbying, and organized crime. The final group of industries will grow dramatically in a networked economy, because people will be able to do these fun things.

Industries Strengthened

Several industries suffer within a money economy because people would really like to use them more if they could. Think of all of the things people would do more if they only had more money. All of those things will become much more popular when people have the economic power to do whatever they like to do.

Education. Many people would like to go to college or just take classes part time but they cannot afford it. Some are teenagers whose families just do not have the money. Some people made the mistake of having children before they finished their education and the costs of raising their own child gets in the way of paying for college, much less paying for the costs of daycare for the child while the parents attend classes. Some are people who want to change careers, or find a career in the first place after spending their early lives floating around from job to job. All of these people will be able to afford to go to school in a networked economy, and the education industry will boom as a result.

Fitness. The fitness industry is another area that will benefit immensely from the transition to a networked economy. The fitness industry includes local indoor exercise clubs, aerobics studios, health spas, massage parlors and yoga centers, and all types of athletic classes like martial arts, dancing, gymnastics, fencing, etc. It also includes outdoor activities that people like to do but which are expensive, like horseback riding, SCUBA diving, golf, skydiving, skiing, and all of the other activities that people like to do but either they cannot afford, or are far away and traveling to the activity site is expensive. All of these activities will be available to everyone and as a result will be even more popular. In a networked economy, all of our health improvement opportunities will be much greater.

Recreation. While some of us think that fitness and recreation are the same thing, there are diversions in this world that do not involve sweating. Sampling the full variety of the human experience can be quite expensive in the money economy and this area too will grow after the transition to a networked economy. From amusement parks and movie theaters, to concerts, the opera and live theater, to boat rides along the waterfront, to tasting the infinite combinations of food and drink in restaurants, bistros, vineyards, and right at home, we will be able to enjoy the joys of life much more in a networked economy.

Manufacturing. As I have written above, only thirty percent of the global economy is fully developed, and only the tiniest percentage of the world population can truly buy everything they need in their lives. That means that at least seventy percent of the population needs more goods and services than they are able to buy in a money economy. At least 70 percent of the population needs more than their current supply of goods and services. Somebody has to manufacture those goods. When demand increases in the networked economy, the manufacturing industries will soak up the unemployed among us. The manufacturing industry will likely go through a revolution of automation very quickly as that industry struggles to keep up with the exploding demand from the population.

Research and Invention. How often do we hear requests for money for a particular field of research, perhaps for a rare disease? It happens quite often … every time we turn on the television, it often seems. The first step in the research process is to find funding for the equipment, the staff, and the facilities for whatever kind of research one wants to undertake. Plenty of avenues of research go unexplored because the limited supply of money can fund only so many discoveries. How many diseases could we have cured? How many problems could we have solved? How many new breakthroughs could we have made if not for this limitation on our lives: the budget constraint? There is no way to know.

In a networked economy, though, our best and brightest will be able to take our state of knowledge as far as their amazing minds can go. There will also be many more researchers in the world to tackle these problems for us, thanks to free universal education around the world in a networked economy. All of the human potential being wasted among populations living in malnourished poverty will be more fully realized in a networked economy.

Inventors, likewise often come up with great ideas but they do not have the funding to pursue the invention all the way through development and marketing. It is true that most inventions are not marketable, but we never know where we will find the next idea that is just crazy enough to work and make everyone's life better, or maybe just more fun. It could be from the mind of that strange, penniless, garage-based inventor down the street.

Services of all Kinds. Aside from the services that we have already listed like masseurs and robot butlers, people will be able to use all kinds of services in their new lives. There will be greater demand for maid service companies, gardeners, carpenters, and even general contractors to help people add that new feature to people's homes, like they have always wanted to. Other services that are strictly for the wealthy in a money economy will expand to the whole population: personal assistants, interior decorators, personal chef services that deliver gourmet dinners to our homes, style consultants, personal concierges, lifestyle coaches, make-up artists, and place holders to stand in line at events like concerts or bureaucratic requirements like the vehicle registration department. All of these services, and many others that I have not listed, will expand dramatically in a world where anyone can afford anything.

Travel and Tourism. The final industry to benefit from a networked economy is the travel and tourism industry. We would all like to take a trip to see a place we have not seen and visit a culture we have not experienced. That will be possible for everyone at any time in a networked economy. Airlines, train companies, bus lines, hotels, resorts, tour companies, and all of the businesses surrounding these companies will see interest in their business' offerings go through the roof when we transition to a networked economy. Let us not forget tourism that literally out of this world expensive right now: space tourism will also be within every person's budget. The sky will not even be the limit of our entertainment and recreation options in a networked economy.

Common Comment: Now, wait a minute! You just listed nine industries that will go out of business, five industries that will fade some, and seven industries that will get bigger in this networked economy of yours.

That is right.

Common Comment: And your networked economy requires everyone to work.

Exactly.

Common Comment: Well, smart guy, will the number of jobs you will gain make up for all of those jobs you just lost?

It is most likely that the exploding demand for manufactured goods and for services of all kinds will far outstrip the available labor even in our vastly underemployed population. The service industry will likely never come to a point where they cannot use more people. This is especially true for the specialty services that are labor intensive, like housecleaning, gardening, or personal chef services for example. Also, the rules of employment that we laid out above create the opportunity for one parent to stay at home to take care of their children. That will lead many dual income homes to take one person out of the labor market to stay home. Many of those single parents out there will also take advantage of the opportunity to stop working and look after their children.

With all of that in mind, I think it is far more likely that this will lead to a revolution in the automation of the economy as a whole. We will see technology step in to make up for a shortage of labor in a very busy economic network. The exploding demand and limited labor, combined with the incentive to automate in the way that we will calculate productive market share in a networked economy, will lead almost certainly to far greater automation in our economy.

In many grocery markets today, for example, we see stores experimenting with self-checkout scanners that enable consumers to scan their own goods, pay, make their own change, bag their own items, and hand themselves their receipt for the purchase. They can even wish themselves to have a good day if they like. Meanwhile, there is often one person overseeing eight or nine registers to resolve any problems. Self-checkout will someday be the normal way a store works and having a person actually bagging a person's groceries will be something reserved for very small stores.

Networked capitalism will create an incentive to automate the economy as much as possible. Over the course of fifty or one hundred years as the economy automates more and more, we can shorten the work day more and more. We may reach a point where the economy is completely automated and each person will only have to work a few hours a week overseeing the machines to keep the economy running. That would be a great long term goal for the economy: to automate as much as possible and require as little human labor as possible, leading to a day when the economy requires very little labor at all.

In any case the labor force will look quite a bit different. Money is a very important part of every aspect of our lives. All of the people whose job it is to manage those various money-centered aspects of our lives will need new jobs. Others for whom money is important but not vital to their jobs will see their industries diminished. And those industries that people would use more if only they had more money will see their industries grow and grow.

Economic Stability

In a networked economy, we will not have to suffer through economic downturns that destroy our savings, throw us into unemployment, and generally cause a lot of misery. The networked economy will also not be catastrophically affected by attacks and natural disasters like a money economy is. This book has made this claim many times: that a networked economy will be stable and not be subject to the recessions and depressions that a money economy suffers through. How can it make that claim?

In a networked economy, there will be no recessions or depressions because there will be no money medium to dramatically change consumer demand depending on whether they are confident they will have money in the future or afraid they will not. Once the networked economy is set up, people will develop eating and living habits based on the new rules of open access to the entire economy. Their economic power will be without limit and consistent across time, the supply will level out at some higher level, and therefore every person's consumption will become more consistent regardless of their life situation. So there will not be wild fluctuations in demand like there are in a money economy. Demand will stabilize at some higher level than it is today, which will stabilize the rate of production, and economic policy will become a matter of logistics: how best do we sustainably produce enough goods and services to meet the needs of the population?

Also, changes in demand and production will not affect the economic power of people and businesses. Returning to the bookstores in our earlier example of competing without money, success for any one of the stores will depend on them maintaining a particular share of the book sales in their market. Overall demand for books might fall for example, perhaps due to rising concern for cutting down trees to make books and the increasing popularity of electronic books. If the decrease affects the whole market the same, sales should fall for everyone, which means they will all keep their market share. However, perhaps shrinking demand does hit one store alone and they need to lay off people, or perhaps the lower overall demand leads a store to believe that they can handle the lower demand with fewer people, which will increase their market share.

If a few of these bookstore workers loses their job, the newly unemployed people will not lose their economic power as we saw in the above rules for unemployment. They will have to live under their community's rules for unemployment, but they will still be able to eat, drink and consume all of the things they need from the economy. Consumption will be completely divorced from the mass psychology of consumer confidence and from economic power overall. People might lose a job they really like and be forced to take a job that they like less, but their economic power will not change. We will all be economically equal. Demand will remain stable, which means supply will be stable, and able to refine its procedures to maximize efficiency.

Better Absorb Catastrophic Attack. In a money economy, everything is relative and everything is connected. A natural disaster or a terrorist strike on a financial center can change consumer confidence and strain a government budget in ways that affect the global economy. The terrorist attacks on New York in September, 2001, for example, caused panic around the nation and around the world, people slowed down their spending, growth in the gross national product slowed, and all of that contributed to the economic recession that soon followed. A single, tragically placed, nuclear weapon could destroy enough of the United States and contaminate enough outside of that area as the radiation spreads to crash our money economy and send a financial panic throughout the world.

In a networked economy, however, there will not be a money system to connect consumption in one part of the world with a tragedy in another part of the world. Economic policy will become a matter of logistics: how much of which goods and services are in demand and how do we sustainably produce enough to meet that demand? A terrorist attack in New York City will economically affect consumers and producers in New York, and the consumption of any goods and services that are made in New York, but they will not effect consumption of, say, Napa Valley wine, which is made in California.

A networked economy will be more resilient in the face of tragedy than a money economy ever could be for the simple reason that the mass psychology of consumer confidence plays such a large role in a money economy. If a networked economy is attacked, people might panic and stock up on supplies, but that change in consumption will not affect the health of the larger global economy. It also will not change the economic power of consumers. The rest of the economy will chug right along until the area of the economy under attack comes back on line and begins producing goods and services again. Remember, the global economy will have the same structure as the internet. When one section of the internet goes offline, the rest of the internet does not even notice.

For all of these reasons, a networked economy will be far more stable and resilient than a money economy could ever be. A networked economy will better serve us if there is a catastrophe. It will serve us better if the environmentalists are correct and global warming causes dramatic changes in our world, like flooding or changes in our food production due to changing weather patterns. It will also serve us better if astronomers and geologists are correct and one of those regularly occurring big asteroids comes our way. Any of these events would have horrible consequences for a money economy but not a networked economy. Less catastrophically, a networked economy will be better able to handle dramatic changes in the workforce, like the mass-retirement of a baby boom generation, or the decline in population that comes with the lower birth rates of a developed, advanced economy.

Higher Quality Goods and Services

Not only will we be able to buy what we want, but the quality of the available products will be dramatically better in a networked economy. In a world where everyone can buy anything they want, what are the chances that they will buy what we now know as "budget" items? By budget items I meet those goods that are lower quality and therefore lower priced.

This means for example the low priced car that gets a person from one point in town to another point in town, but does not have the latest electronic gadgets, the heated seats, the navigation software, the remote starter, or even the remote door lock. Who will buy this car when they can buy any car on the lot? If someone can buy any brand they wish, they will naturally buy the best brand they can find. So, if everyone goes after the best item on the market, what will all of the other brands do? They will increase their quality to compete or they will go out of business as their market share plummets.

As a result, the overall quality of goods and services across the economy will increase as they all fight to attract the unfettered demand of the population. It will become as if every store in the world is catering to the wealthiest people in the world, who can go anywhere else to get what they need. In fact, that will be true of every one of their customers, because we will all have that exact power. Over time as each product line, each service, and each industry competes to attract absolutely powerful customers, the quality of the overall economy will just keep on improving and improving.

Less Litigation

After working and investing responsibly, lawsuits may be the most effective way to make money in a modern capitalist economy. The United States has become a more and more litigious nation to the point where filing a lawsuit at the least provocation has become a cliché that is as true as it is sad. In a networked economy, the only benefit to suing someone will be to establish blame. The winner of a lawsuit will gain no economic benefit from the lawsuit. Therefore, unless there is a crime involved and prison time is an option, there will be no need for courts and lawyers to be involved in accidents.

If a person gets into a car accident, both cars will go to the garage to be fixed at no charge to either person. Of course if one person intentionally runs over another person, that is a criminal matter and the courts will get involved. If a person accidentally slips and falls on a wet floor, the hospital will fix their broken arm at no charge. So there is no need to sue the owner of the building. In a networked economy one person cannot hurt another person financially, so there will be no reason for a court to decide who is financially liable. And since there will be nothing to gain financially from a lawsuit, there will be fewer of them.

Fewer Crimes

In a networked economy, we will all be safer, because there will be less crime. Money, or more specifically greed, is a big motivator for committing crimes. However, there are plenty of other motivations for crime including hatred, jealousy, insanity, envy, crimes of passion, and crimes to obtain power, among others. All of those other motivations will still exist in a networked economy and therefore there will still be crime in a networked economy.

If the reader is interested in the subject of money and crime, back in July of 1992, James Coleman wrote an excellent article called "Crime and Money" where he wrote:

> Although we have examined several ways by which the use of money encourages particular types of criminal behavior, this conclusion may not appear to have many practical consequences. We are obviously not going to

> reduce the role of the monetary economy in our social system in order to bring down the crime rate.[35]

To which I say, "Let's do it!" Seriously, though, it is obvious that greed leads some people to commit crimes in a money economy.

Networked capitalism will make the old saying "Crime doesn't pay" an absolute fact. One of the worst things about money is that it can be used for any purpose, whether it is a wonderful purpose, an evil purpose, or a completely mundane every day purpose. When the economy is a big network, the society will be able to choose who has access to the network and who does not. This means that economic power will only come from legitimate, legal activities. People and businesses who contribute to the economy in a legitimate way will have unlimited access to the economy. There will still be crime in a networked economy, of course, but there will be no economic incentive for it. In a networked economy, a person can only gain economic power by working for an accredited business, so money related crimes will be abolished.

That means the illicit industries, like the drug trade will also suffer in a networked economy, because drug cartels are not accredited businesses. People have always sought to alter their state of mind, and that will not change. However, making and distributing illegal drugs will no longer offer any economic benefit, and gangs will no longer be able to fund armies by selling addiction to children around the world. The drug industry will collapse when we move to a networked economy and drug making and distribution will become more local and voluntary.

Some crimes will be abolished by definition because they are by definition money crimes. Bribery, fraud, embezzlement, counterfeiting, gambling, and bookmaking will all be abolished because by definition, they are money crimes. Prostitution will also be abolished because it is defined as selling sex for money. Out of the millions of arrests each year in the United States, about four percent of them are for offenses that will be abolished when we move to a networked economy.

Other types of crimes will be diminished by the transition to a networked economy. Property crimes for example will be seriously

---

[35] Coleman 1992, p. 834. See also Simmel, 1907, p. 432 on money and "mean machinations" as he calls them: "We resent the money economy offering its central value as a fully compliant instrument for the meanest machinations."

diminished because when anybody can walk into any store and walk out with whatever they need, there is little reason to steal from somebody else. That does not let rare property like fine art and rare gems off the hook of course. Crimes that will be diminished include robbery, burglary, larceny theft, motor vehicle theft, and the buying, receiving, and possession of stolen property. These crimes make up about fourteen percent of all arrests in a money economy. In total, nearly twenty percent of crime will be abolished or seriously diminished when we switch to a networked economy. Other crimes will decrease as well if for no other reason than in a moneyless economy, people's lives will be better, less stressful, and they will find fewer reasons to commit crimes.

I listed bribery above, and specifically political corruption will decrease in a networked economy because we will all be financially equal, including those despised politicians. As discussed above, politicians will not need to spend all of their time raising money because campaigning will become free just like everything else. That means that individuals and interest groups will not be able to buy influence by contributing money to politicians' campaign funds or by giving money directly to the politicians. Interest groups will have to go back to influencing policy based on the number of members they have instead of how much campaign money they contribute. That is the proper order of things.

* * *

That will be life in a networked economy. We will all be able to consume whatever we need, which means that we will have to be even more careful not to use up our resources by consuming ourselves out of a planet. Participating in our government will be even more important because the government will not have a budget constraint either. We will be able to focus more on real, meaningful things in our lives because money worries will not interfere with our lives, our dreams, or our relationships. Greed will not be such a big part of our culture in a networked economy.

Nine industries that exist because of money will become obsolete and five industries that exist largely because of money will be diminished, leading to a smaller job base and perhaps a shorter workweek for all of us. The industries that manufacture goods and provide us with fun activities will grow and thrive when everyone can afford to enjoy more of their products. Our lives will not be rocked and buffeted by economic recessions and catastrophic events in a networked economy. Finally, there will be less litigation and fewer crimes, since people will not be able to gain financially by suing someone or by stealing their belongings. Overall, our lives will be easier, more stable and safer, and our society will be calmer in a networked economy.

Chapter 6

Conclusion

Every economy everywhere, in every time period, is a system for using the resources of the environment to meet the needs of the community. The question is: what is the best system to do that? Throughout our history, people have tried many different arrangements. We currently use money to organize our economy and until recently it has been the best technology invented for the job. To acquire goods and services, every person and every business needs money to pay for them. The need for money is the engine that drives the economy.

A money capitalist economy with an uncorrupted, open marketplace is by far the best type of economy that has ever been invented. It is a dynamic, adaptive economy that responds to the evolving needs of the community. Since the marketplace is uncorrupted, the government mostly stays out of the way of business and enables goods, services, and labor to flow throughout the economy. It also uses our natural self-interest as an engine to drive production and innovation, which gives people and businesses a reason to participate in the economy. No other type of economy has accomplished this as well as money capitalism does.

The money capitalist economy, however, is not perfect. The first big problem we need to solve is the budget constraint caused by the limited supply of money, which holds back production and makes the economy inefficient at meeting the needs of the population. Because we all need money to get what we need from the economy, the economy will only produce what we can pay for. Mining companies, farmers, lumber companies and other companies that take resources from nature only take as many resources as they can sell. This would be fine if we all had plenty of money, but every person, every business, and every government suffers from a shortage of money.[36] Only thirty percent of the global economy is fully developed. The other seventy percent of the economy could be providing us with a great deal more goods, services, and labor.

Not only that, even when a developed money economy is growing healthily, one in eight people still live in poverty. No matter how good the money economy is chugging along, no matter how prosperous the society is, there is always a section of the population living in poverty. Anti-poverty programs can move resources to these people, but funding for these programs is always a hot button political issue, which makes funding sporadic and unreliable. It would be far more efficient if the system enabled every person to have access to the bounty of nature without the need for charity.

This persistent poverty is bad news for poor people and poor nations, and it is bad news for the rest of us, too. First, living in poverty leads to less education and wastes whatever potential a poor person has to benefit the rest of us with the product of their labor, whatever solutions they might find to the problems we all face in our lives and the desperation of poverty harms the rest of us with an increased crime rate. Second, there are many things that we all want to do, places we want to go, many problems that we could solve, diseases that we could cure, and discoveries that we could find for want of more money to pay for it all. All of our lives will be better when we network the global economy, get rid of the budget constraint, and use the full resources of the environment to satisfy our needs.

The second problem with the money economy is its volatility. When people spend their money freely, and more money flows through our economy, the economy grows, companies hire people, and more people have the money to buy what they need. When people get concerned about their future or the future of their money supply, they slow down their spending. That causes a contraction in production leading to people losing their jobs and the general spread of economic misery. We call this the business cycle and it is an unfortunate reality that we have learned to live with. It controls our lives and decides our happiness and prosperity far too much. As we have seen recently, a big dip in the economy can wipe out retirement savings, businesses, and

---

[36] "The general misery of human life is most fully reflected … by the constant shortage of money under which most people suffer." Simmel, 1907, p. 120.

countless dreams. Thanks to information technology and a worldwide internet, however, the business cycle is an unnecessary burden.

We have the technology to stabilize the economy, get rid of the budget constraint, open up the economy to everyone, feed the world, and more easily spread capitalism to developing nations. We can turn the global economy into one big economic network that we all contribute to. In return for our contribution to the economy, we will all have unlimited access to the economy and be able to buy whatever we need.

Businesses will increase their production to meet this increased demand and we will use the internet to coordinate competition between businesses, which will compete for consumers' business based on how many units they sell instead of how much money they make. Businesses will compete with other similar businesses to maintain and improve their share of their particular market. If they cannot maintain a minimum market share, they will lose their business license and be forced to close.

Businesses will adapt to changing public desires in order to maintain their market share and keep their business license. People will compete to do the work that they truly enjoy and they will work hard to keep those jobs. Taking money out of the economy and networking economic competition will enable all consumers to demand what they need from the economy and it will enable producers to extract more from the environment to increase production and meet that need.

This new networked economy will enable all of us to live our lives, raise our children, and retire comfortably without worrying about money. It will enable developing nations around the world to create vibrant, competitive economies that will feed, clothe, entertain, and educate their populations.

We will still use our natural self-interest to drive the economy. Businesses will be forced to evolve to maintain their market share when their competitors come up with some innovation in their products or practices that draw more customers. People will strive to find jobs that they truly enjoy and they will compete for the best jobs with the best opportunities and newest advantageous challenges.

We will manage this new economy by converting two existing money-related institutions into organizations that measure the value of our contributions to the economy, and provide us with the accreditation to have full access to the economy. Individuals and their dependents will have full access to the economy as long as they are employed by an accredited business. Banks will be used to store employment information and to communicate that information to merchants on behalf of the consumers who want to acquire merchants' goods and services.

We will set up an employment verification network very similar to our current credit card verification network for people to use when they buy goods and services, and the process of buying something will look very similar. Consumers will choose their items from the store shelves and bring them to the counter, where the clerk will scan the items for inventory control purposes. The consumer will hand over a bank card that will look a great deal like today's credit cards. The bank card will be a plastic card with a magnetic strip that the consumer's bank will issue to them. The clerk will swipe the card through a reader and the consumer will punch in a personal identification number into the keypad to verify their identity. The reader will electronically verify the consumer's employment with the bank and the consumer will take the goods home with them.

The process will look the same if the person is in a store buying goods, in a hospital receiving care, in a massage parlor getting the stress worked out of their muscles, or in a beach resort ordering another frosted drink from the waiter. The process will look the same if the person is in their home town, across the country, or across the world. The internet will link the global economy and enable every person to get what they need from the economy.

Businesses will have full access to the economy as long as they maintain a minimum share of their market. Each business' value to the economy will be measured by making them compete with similar businesses based on how many products they sell. We will keep track of competition between businesses by converting our tax collection agencies into competition measurement offices (CMOs) that will collect sales data from businesses, compare the sales data to similar businesses, and publish the market share for each business.

The rules of competition will be determined by local law in each state and each nation. When the networked economy is being implemented, every business will get together with its direct competitors and create rules that they will compete under. Those rules will be approved and enforced by their Competition Measurement Office. The rules will set a minimum market share that each business will have to maintain. If they fall below that market share they will be given a year to raise their market share, and if they cannot raise their market share they will lose access to the economy and be forced to close.

The rules will set businesses against each other by requiring every business to maintain a share of the market equal to a certain percentage of the market leader's share. As smaller businesses take business away from the market leader and each other, it will lower the minimum for everyone, creating an incentive for smaller businesses to innovate. Productivity can be maintained by measuring market share in terms of average sales per hour worked per employee. This will force businesses to create as money goods and services as possible with as little labor as possible, which is the goal of any economy.

This will set up a vibrant competition between businesses where new businesses and businesses with less market share will innovate to increase their market share and make their business more secure in the economy. Then the market leaders will have to innovate to keep up with the innovations of the other businesses. The global economy will be a constantly evolving marketplace where businesses compete for consumer attention, and consumers decide which businesses succeed and which businesses fail.

We will implement this new economy slowly. The networked economy, in the simplest terms, is an alternative accounting system, so it can be set up and tested while the money economy is still running. We can first set it up in a test nation and run it along side their money economy for a few years to work out any bugs. Then, after a test period they will stop using money and the world will support the test nation, providing it with whatever goods and services they demand. This will enable us to test how much people will consume when they can consume anything. If after a few years the test reveals that the networked economy has some fatal flaw we have not foreseen, they can start using their money again and we will either fix the problem or forget about the idea. If the test is a success, we will start implementing the networked economy in the rest of the world.

Once we make the decision to start create a networked economy, it will take between ten and twenty years to complete the process of creating the infrastructure to coordinate a networked economy, writing all of the rules and laws, testing it in a test nation along side of their money economy, transitioning the test nation fully to a networked economy, then setting up the infrastructure in the rest of the world and testing it along side their money economy, and then finally ceasing the use of money and then transitioning fully to a networked economy everywhere.

The steps in the implementation process are:

1. Develop networks and software programs to run the system.
2. Legislatures will rewrite their criminal codes to create non-money fines for minor violations of the law.
3. Local governments will create the Bank/CMO network to keep track of and communicate employment, supply and demand. Once we create that network, businesses around the world will create the rules that they will compete under, and CMOs around the world will review all of those sets of rules.
4. Banks will issue bank cards to everyone and educate them how to use them.
5. We will test the system, running it along side of the money economy for two years to work out any bugs.
6. When the networked economy is fully tested as a ghost system running along side the money economy, and we decide to really go for it, producers around the world will increase production to meet the increased demand that people will have when they can buy anything.
7. When everything is in place and tested, stores have the increased inventory to handle the increased demand, and everyone knows what is going to happen, we can discontinue the money economy.

Once we complete the transition to a networked economy, our lives will be easier and the world will be a much better place. We can stop worrying and thinking about money all of the time and focus on what is really important in life: taking care of our families, enjoying our lives, and chasing our dreams. If we want something from the store we will be able to get it. Whatever recreation, travel, dining options, or sports we want to try will be free to us. If we get sick or have an accident, medical care and mechanical care will be freely available. Serious accidents and permanent disabilities will no longer strain the lifestyles of our families. When we reach retirement age, we will be able to retire if we want to, without worrying about running out of money before we die. When we reach an age where we need care around the clock, we will be able to have excellent care without burdening our families financially.

We will not have to worry about an economic recession coming along and throwing our families into hard times, because the economy will be much more stable and resilient. The networked economy will not have boom and bust cycles because the growth in production will no longer rely on the volume of money flowing through our economy. Economic life in one part of the world will no longer be affected by catastrophes in another part of the world because the mass psychology of consumer confidence will not play such a big part in the health of the economy. The networked economy will be much easier to export to undeveloped areas because the structure will be purely logistical. There will be no money economy to nurture and grow like over-sensitive slime in a Petri dish.

The goods and services that are available to all of us will grow in number and in quality. All kinds of services will be available to everyone, which will lead to an explosion in demand for services that are currently reserved for the wealthiest among us. When anyone can afford any good or service, all goods and services will have to increase their quality in order to attract consumer interest and maintain their market share. We will also mandate an increase in the lifespan of the many goods that can be bought in an effort to expand their use, make them recyclable, decrease the pace that we have to take resources from the environment, and make it easier to provide as much as possible to the entire population.

There will also be less crime and fewer lawsuits once greed is removed as a motivation for committing crimes and filing lawsuits. Crimes that are by definition money crimes, or crimes with money, will be abolished. These include bribery, fraud, embezzlement, counterfeiting, gambling, bookmaking, and prostitution. Other crimes will be diminished when there is no economic benefit to committing them, like property crimes and drug crimes. Political corruption will be minimized when interest groups and criminals cannot give elected officials any commodity that will benefit them economically.

The End.

That is the story of how we can take away everyone's money worries, stabilize the economy, spread affluence throughout the world, and move beyond this era of greed and division. We can stop the endless fighting over money and scarce resources, and really develop as a society. We can also spread affluence to the whole world. I look forward to the day when every land is the land of plenty.

A final question I often get from this idea is, "This is crazy. Do you really think this is going to happen?" The answer is I do not know. Democracy was once a crazy idea. Going to the moon was once a crazy idea. Flying was once a crazy idea. Once upon a time we relied on spears to hunt, and killing animals from a distance was a crazy idea. If history teaches us anything, it is that change is the only constant and people always use new technologies to improve their lives.

Is it possible to organize a global economy without money? Absolutely. Should we? I think so. The first step in making a change is to come up with an alternative. Here it is. If you agree that we should use the internet to stabilize the economy and make all of our lives better, join this new movement, spread the idea about networked capitalism, call and write your government representative, and let's do it. Thank you for reading my book. Please stop by the website for the latest developments: www.FixingCapitalism.com.

Index: Frequently Asked Questions

General Questions:

The following is a compiled listing of the frequently asked questions and comments, which were sprinkled throughout the text.

Is this communism?

This is capitalism. This is about open, decentralized markets and vibrant, creative competition between businesses. The cold war is over and capitalism won! Communism is dead as a theory for managing large economies. Even the old communist nations are not so communist anymore. This is a new idea, not communism or traditional capitalism. It is the next step in the evolution of capitalism, where private property is still traded in an open market, according to the rules of supply and demand. The difference is that the exchange will be networked and coordinated with the internet instead of mediated with money. This will stabilize the economy, prevent recessions and depressions, and enable the economy to increase production dramatically to efficiently meet everyone's needs.

I love making money just as much as the next guy. I used to be a wealth manager after all. Please don't hate me for it. I never promised my clients more than I could deliver. However, in spite of loving money, I know that we can manage our economy better. I am a little like the Ferrari driver who knows that a fuel-efficient Tesla will also stimulate the senses, without spewing pollution in the air. The money economy works just fine for me and maybe twenty percent of humanity. While it is working for some of us, though, it is doing damage to many other people and places. Plus, now I know that there is a better way for me and everyone else to get all of those great things out of the economy. This will bring affluence to the world, make us all safer, and be better for everyone in the long run.

My job when I worked in investments was to make other people wealthy. If we do this right, we can make everyone wealthy.

Everyone around the world can feel the real wealth of a comfortable, healthy lifestyle where they can dream their dreams, work to realize those dreams, raise their families, and then retire in peace. Networked capitalism will be a decentralized market economy, not communism.

Communism, just to really address the question, is a centrally controlled economy,[37] where the government bureaucracy decides what goods are made and how much variety people have. As I said above, networked capitalism will be a decentralized market economy. The internet will coordinate exchange, and everyday people like you and me will control the economy with our decisions about which products we like and do not like, just like we do in a capitalist money economy. The role of government will actually go down when they will no longer control how much we can buy through changes in the interest rates or the tax rates.

The government also will no longer be in the business of redistributing wealth, so all of those departments that exist to take money from tax payers and give services to the poor will be closed. Do you like the idea of smaller government? The government will be a lot smaller and less intrusive in a networked capitalist economy. Networked capitalism will spell an end to the era of the welfare state, which is good news for everyone out the who disagrees

Then it is socialism, that's for sure!

It is not socialism either. Socialism is government ownership of land and property for the public good. All of the goods and services in the networked economy, including real estate, will be privately owned. Of course there will still be public land and property like parks, highways, sewer systems and the like, which are used for the public good and are therefore technically socialistic. However, networked capitalism is an economic system where private property is traded in an open market according to the rules of supply and demand, with minimal government interference.

---

[37] See Milton Friedman, 1962, p. 13: "Fundamentally, there are only two ways of coordinating the economic activities of millions. One is central direction involving the use of coercion—the technique of the Army and of the modern totalitarian state. The other is voluntary cooperation of individuals—the technique of the market place." Networked Capitalism will be a market economy that coordinates the voluntary cooperation of free individuals.

More importantly, though, this book is not about ideology; it is about technology. My conservative friends like that we are going to shrink the government and make the capitalist economy stable. Nobody likes the government interfering in our lives, and when they no longer feel the need to counter the inequalities of money capitalism, the government will have to close all of those bureaucracies, and they will have less of a role in our lives. We could shrink the United States government down to the size it was before World War II and all of the government programs of the welfare state.

Conservatives also do not like the wild boom-and-crash fluctuations that a money economy goes through. Recessions cost us money and are dangerous to all our well-being. Even those who invest only in bonds did not like it that some bond markets froze up during the Great Recession and they could not sell their bonds when they wanted to sell. The networked economy will be a system of production and distribution that we never have to worry about. We will be able to live our lives in financial peace and equality, just like we now live in political peace and equality.

My progressive friends like it that the economy will benefit everyone. They like reading the Declaration of Independence and seeing it written there that we are all created equal. They like the idea that America is a land where everyone is free and equally able to pursue their life, liberty and happiness as they see fit, and they know everyone's lack of money gets in the way of those supposedly inalienable rights. Moving to a networked economy is the key to making that a reality for everyone around the world.

Both groups like it that the crime rate will go down. Crime will not pay in a networked economy because we will have the power to decide who has access to the economic network. In networked capitalism, economic power will come from either owning an accredited business, or working for one. There will no longer be a medium of exchange that bad people can use for bad purposes. Drug cartels will have nothing economically to gain from distributing addiction. All of the money related crimes like bribery, fraud, embezzlement, prostitution, counterfeiting, etc. will go extinct when we get rid of money.

We will finally be able to put aside the nonstop fighting over money, taxes, and spending in our political debates, and really develop as a society. Remember back in the mid-twentieth century when technology was going to solve all of our problems? We were all going to fly around with jetpacks, nuclear energy would be too cheap to meter, there would be no poverty, and everyone would have robot butlers? Well, last year an engineer from New Zealand introduced what may be the first commercially viable jetpack. This year I am introducing a way to get rid of poverty and help every kid afford a robot butler. So, we are getting there!

This new adaptation to the capitalist economy is just that, a technological adaptation. It is not a conservative adaptation or a progressive adaptation. It will not prove one side right and the other side wrong. The economy is just a tool. The economy can be used for conservative ends or progressive ends. It is just an economy. It will more efficiently take the resources of the environment and use them to meet our needs. Networking capitalism will solve a lot of problems, but do not worry; we will have plenty more problems left behind.

But who will control this networked economy, then?

The economy will be controlled by the same people who control the internet: nobody. A good economy functions on its own, without anybody trying to wrestle it down and force it to fulfill one goal or another. Networked capitalism will be a good economy. The internet will be used to coordinate exchange, measure supply and demand, and keep track of the competitive economy. It will be how we express our economic desires, just like we now hand over money to express demand for a good or service. Once we develop rules for the competition between businesses, the economy will function on its own without government interference or control by special interests, which is the way it should be. State and local governments will be in charge of compiling and publishing the sales data that will be used to measure competition and determine which businesses succeed or fail, but that will be more of an accounting role.

How can you have capitalism without money? Capitalism is the quest for money and it is impossible to have capitalism without money. If you take money out of the economy, you no longer have capitalism, so you cannot call what you have created networked "capitalism". I don't know what you would call it but this name is not accurate.

That is an absolutely fair point. Many people find the idea of capitalism without money a contradiction in terms.[38] Capital-ism is after all an economy centered on the use of capital, *i.e.* money.

Technically that is true but if you look at it there are really four parts to a traditional money capitalist economy, the first being privately owned property, which provides the fuel for economic innovation. The primal human statement, "I want that" leads to economic demand for whatever "that" is, which drives the market to innovate to meet that demand with more of that product. The alternative statement, "I don't want that" likewise leads to the end of products, services and business as the market rejects an obsolete market offering. I will not dwell on private ownership first because everyone understands what private ownership is. The concept of "this is mine" is very straight forward. Second, this will not change between a money economy and a networked economy. We trade private property today in the money economy and we will trade private property in a networked economy.

The second part of the capitalist economy is an open market, where anyone can bring a good or a service to offer for sale. This is an amazingly democratic invention, these open markets. Any person with a product can offer it to the market. We do not have to pay off some bureaucrat to file our corporation papers with the secretary of state, or the department of corporations, in our state. We do not need special permission from some politician. The governor of the state does not use political pressure to squeeze his friends' business competitors out of the market to put more money in his friends' pockets, who would then of course put money in the governor's pockets. The market is open to all comers. They do not even have to be citizens of the country, as is evident by the guys standing outside of moving van rental companies, offering their strong backs to anyone who makes an offer.

Open markets do not exist in many places around the world and doing business in economies that are not open is a very different experience. Bribes for bureaucrats and corrupt officials have to be budgeted in to the cost of creating a project or a business enterprise in

[38] Most notably, every dictionary that exists. Schumpeter (1991, p. 313) wrote that the necessary elements of capitalism were private property and credit markets. I could logically stretch the definition of credit to fit inside of a networked economy, since credit is little more than confidence in a person's future economic power. We will all have unending economic power in a networked economy.

a limited market. Political corruption is always a concern and being on the right side of the local government is very important or a business owner may arrive to work one morning and find his business smoldering in flames. Or he may arrive to work and then never be seen again. Organized crime is also a constant concern, and managers have to make decisions about whether to pay protection money to the criminals, or more money to the local police as protection from the criminals, or increase security to protect themselves, or all of the above.

An uncorrupted open market is a luxury that we take for granted in the United States, but we should not. It is a wonderful thing that we should all be very thankful for. As much as we all hate paying taxes, we should be very thankful for the open, uncorrupted business environment that our taxes pay to maintain.

The third part of capitalist trade is the law of supply and demand. Most people think of supply and demand as it applies to changes in the price of a good or service that is for sale. If there is less supply, the price is higher because people have to pay more money for a scarce commodity. If there is greater demand, the price is higher because people are willing to pay more for a commodity that is very popular. If there is greater supply or less demand, the prices are lower for the reverse reasons.

However, think of what supply and demand does for the economy socially, on a structural basis. Supply and demand decides the success or failure of every business or product. The best part of this system is that it puts the decision about which products succeed and which ones fail into the hands of the consumer. The products that attract consumer demand succeed. The products that do not attract consumer demand fail. That is very democratic! This is what makes a capitalist economy dynamic, responding to the latest technologies and the ever-evolving needs of the population.

This concept of supply and demand, where the individual decisions by consumers combine to determine what directions the economy goes, is absolutely essential to a dynamic economy. Some people who are fond of either Karl Marx or the utopian ideas of anarchy often ask why we needed competition at all. They would say that we only need one kind of peanut butter after all. A modern, dynamic economy absolutely requires competition between products and services. Without it, the economy would stagnate. That one brand of something might be good now, but what if someone thinks of an innovation that people will like better? Without competition, the better brand would never be realized.

The fourth part of the capitalist economy is money, an artificial medium of exchange that we must acquire before we can acquire anything else. The limited supply of money hinders the economy's ability to produce enough goods and services for everyone because the economy can only produce what people have the money to pay for. Greed for money creates poverty because when a limited valuable commodity like money is sought by everyone, there will naturally be people who end up with very little of it. Using a money commodity also creates instability by causing the economy to boom when people spend a lot of money and shrinking the economy into recessions when people save their money instead of spending. The realities of money also contribute to envy, division, hatred, war, and endless crime and treachery.

Obviously, the point here is that we should keep the uncorrupted open market competition, trading private property according to the rules of supply and demand, and get rid of the medium of distribution. Is this capitalism without capital? If we have four social structures that together create a capitalist economy and we keep three of the structures, can we call the new economy a modified capitalist economy? I obviously think so. Since the modification is that we coordinate open market exchange with an information network instead of a money network, I think it is fair to call it networked capitalism.

That is getting to be an academic question about semantics, though. We can debate that all day and night if we like, along with how many angels can fit on the head of a pin. In the meantime, this book is more concerned about what this innovation will do, namely stabilize the economy and make all of our lives better. I think networked capitalism should be the next step in the evolution of capitalism and we have the technology to make it possible.

Would this really work?

This is a very important question, because if it would not work, there is no reason to do it. Let us break that question down into two smaller questions: "Is this an economy?" and "Is this economy democratic?"

<u>Is this an Economy</u>? This is an important question, because we need to know that the system we have designed does everything that

an economy is supposed to do. Nigel Dodd analyzed the role that the monetary network serves in our economy. Since we want to replace that network, the networked economy should perform all of the same functions that the monetary network fulfills. Here are Dodd's five abstract properties of a monetary network:

1. "The network will contain a standardized accounting system into which each monetary form within the network is divisible, enabling its exchange with anything priced in terms of that system."
2. "Money is accepted as payment almost solely on the assumption that it can be re-used later on."
3. "The network will depend on information regarding its spatial characteristics: limits placed on the territory in which" it can be used.
4. "The network is based on legalistic information, usually in the form of rules."
5. "Anyone in possession of money must be able to anticipate, as a matter of routine, its re-use" with other people across the territory.[39]

How does the networked economy match up?

First, does it include a standardized accounting system that enables the exchange of any good or service? Yes. The network has a mechanism for including every person, either as a working consumer, or the dependent of a working consumer, in the economy. Any business can register with their local competition measurement office to hire consumers to create their good or service, and to offer their goods and services to the public. There is no limitation on what goods and services can be offered to the public, other than the fact that they must be legal to possess and exchange. No illegal drugs, heavy firearms, or weapons of mass destruction.

Second, can people trust that the method of exchange will be available today, tomorrow, next year and beyond? Yes. Once the system is set up, it will be enforced and maintained by the governments of the world, just as the money system is maintained today. Of course the governments' role in maintaining the economy

---

[39] Dodd, 1994, p. xxiv. Dalton, 1971, pp. 1-25 provides a similar typology.

will be severely diminished when there are no more taxes to collect and redistribute, financial institutions to regulate and inspect, or interest rates to monitor and adjust. The government will be reduced to the role of accountant, adding up sales data, determining market share, and publishing the results. However, people will have full faith that the system will last when it is backed by the full faith and support of the world community.

Third, will there be clear information about the spatial limitations of the networked economy? Yes. Businesses will know their rules of competition, which will be determined and maintained by each local area. As businesses expand to cover larger areas, they will have to register with the larger competition measurement office. Individuals will have spatial limitations about where they can buy what they need from the economy only if there are nations that choose not to network their economies. Every nation that is on the economic network will fully benefit its citizens and enable them to acquire whatever they need.

Fourth, will the network consist of clear rules that carry the weight of law to determine how economic exchange will take place? Yes. The rules for employment, unemployment, and competition between businesses will be determined and enforced by local governments. Those rules will be clearly communicated to everyone.

Fifth, will people be able to trust that they will be able to acquire what they need from any business in the network across town, across the country, and across the world? Yes. Every person will be to get what they need from every business in every nation around the globe.

Is it Democratic? Networked capitalism looks like it will do all of the things that an economy is supposed to do. Will the new networked economy be democratic? Will it be a fair distribution of economic power that will benefit every person in the society? Luckily the eminent political scientist from Yale University, Robert Dahl outlined what a democratic distribution of power within an association of people would look like. Of course he is talking about government and we are talking about economics, so here is a guide for converting from one to the other: policies=products, votes=purchases, the association=the economy, agenda=marketplace and adoption=deemed a success. I put the economic word in brackets to help the reader understand how this applies to economics.

1. *Effective Participation.* Before a policy [product] is adopted [deemed a success] by the association [economy], all the

members must have equal and effective opportunities for making their views known to the other members as to what the policy [product] should be.

2. *Voting [Purchasing] Equality*. When the moment arrives at which the decision about a policy [product] will finally be made, every member must have an equal and effective opportunity to vote [purchase], and all votes [purchases] must be counted as equal.

3. *Enlightened Understanding*. Within reasonable limits as to time, each member must have equal and effective opportunities for learning about the relevant alternative policies [products] and their likely consequences.

4. *Control of the Agenda [Marketplace]*. The members must have the exclusive opportunity to decide how and, if they choose, what matters [products] are to be placed on the agenda [marketplace]. Thus the democratic process required by the three preceding criteria is never closed. The policies [products] of the association [economy] are always open to change by the members, if they so choose.

5. *Inclusion of Adults*. All, or at any rate most, adult permanent residents should have the full rights of citizens that are implied by the first four criteria.[40]

Will networked capitalism be democratic?

First, before a product is deemed a success or failure, will every member of the community have the equal opportunity to purchase that item if they choose? In other words, when a business is created and a good or service is offered to the marketplace, will every person be able to buy that product if they choose? Yes. Businesses will have at least one year to establish themselves within the marketplace before they have to live by the rules of competition for their area. Also, every person will have unlimited economic power to buy what they want from the economy.

Second, will every purchase be counted equally when determining which products succeed and which products fail? Yes. Every purchase will be added up, and counted only once, to determine an overall level of sales for that product. Those sales will be compared

---

[40] Dahl, 1998, pp. 37-38.

to the sales of other similar products to determine the market share for each product.

Third, will every person have enough time to learn about various products in the marketplace, and buy whichever products they prefer before the products are deemed a success or failure? Yes. Every business will have at least one year to make themselves known in the marketplace and every consumer will have that time to learn about new products and decide whether or not to purchase them.

Fourth, will the market be open to new products and will every person have the ability to bring a new product to the marketplace if they choose? Yes. Every person will have the economic power to create a business and offer whatever products they choose to the marketplace. Starting a business will be free, as will buying the inventory to stock the business. Every person in the world economic network will be completely free to bring their products to the marketplace and then remove those products when they choose.

The second part of this point is if the community decides that they no longer like a product, is there a mechanism for the product to be removed from the marketplace? Yes. Businesses will have to maintain a particular share of their market. As long as a business attracts enough consumers, they will be able to keep their business license and maintain access to the network of suppliers that they need to stock their businesses. If consumers do not patronize the business, the business will lose their license and lose access to the network, and they will be unable to acquire the supplies needed to keep their business running. It is up to consumers to maintain support for a given product, or withdraw that support and force it to close. Therefore, consumers will have equal and exclusive control over the marketplace.

Fifth, will every adult have access to the marketplace and be equally able to exercise the four previous rights? Yes. Not only will every adult have full and equal access to the economy, but every person of every age will have access by their status as either an employed person or a dependent of an employed person or the state for disabled or institutionalized consumers. Dependents will include children, the retired, the disabled, and one parent of a school-aged child.

Therefore, by these measurements, not only will it work, but this is the holy grail of economic innovations: a stable, competitive, democratic economy that will benefit everyone and adapt to the changing needs of the society. Reformers and revolutionaries have been seeking economic democracy for hundreds of years and thanks to the invention of the internet and its instantaneous, global communication of value, economic democracy, *i.e.* universally equal economic freedom, is finally possible for the human race.

Employment –Related Questions

Wait a minute! You mean that if I have a job, I can walk into any store and walk out with whatever I want?

You will have to go through the checkout line so the store can keep track of what you are taking and replenish their inventory, but that is right. Whatever you want, you can take. As a person who contributes to the economic network, you will have a right to full access to all of the goods and services available inside of the network. That will be the right of every person who contributes to the economy as well as their dependents.

That makes no sense. If people can take whatever they want, they will walk out with the whole store and then you won't have a store!

Why will they do that? Think about that for a moment. What will they do with all of those products? Say they drove a big eighteen-wheeled truck to the front door of the grocery store, opened up the back of the truck, went into the grocery store and started carrying out the whole inventory of the store, loading it into the back of the truck. So when they are finished, they have a big truck full of all kinds of fruits and vegetables, canned goods, pasta, soups, fresh meats, milk and dairy products, boxed cereals, books and magazines, all kinds of candy and snack foods, that overpriced hardware equipment that some stores sell, cleaning products, etc. This person drives away with all of these things in the back of the big truck. What will they do with it?

They will sell it! Won't they?

To who? Think about it. They pull the truck down the street or even drive across the country. They park on the side of the road and flip open the back of the truck. Are they going to stand their at the back of the truck with a megaphone and start calling to the crowd? "Get your fresh beef here! We have some wonderful meat here, folks! Step right up to my refrigerated truck and buy all of the groceries you need."

Remember *everybody* can go in to any store and get whatever they want. The whole global economy is one big network where every person has full access to the network. They can have what ever they want out of real, air-conditioned stores that they have been going to for years, where they have clean floors, and plenty of room to browse the shelves for whatever products they might need. If you could walk into any grocery store and get as much food as you wanted, would you get food from some creepy guy with food in the back of his truck?

OK, they wouldn't sell it. But, they would fill up their houses. What about electronics? People will get a hundred flat-screen televisions for their houses.

The chapter on living in a networked economy discusses what will happen to greed when everyone can own anything. We return to the restaurant metaphor and the "all-you-can-eat" establishment. Does a person pile up several plates at the all-you-can-eat buffet, eat a little and then throw the rest out? No. When people can have whatever they want, they take what they need and then leave the rest.

There might be some people who will go crazy with the gadgets, but most people will not. Think about it this way. If we network the global economy and enable every person to buy whatever they need freely, we are basically making everyone like billionaires. They can buy whatever they want. Does a billionaire have piles and piles of electronics in their homes? Have you seen those television shows on all the time that take the viewers for a tour through wealthy people's homes? The homes are not piled to the rafters with television sets. They were elegantly decorated with fine furnishings. They had their supercharged toys and, true, some people had vast collections of expensive things like classic cars, art, or old jewels, like *Faberge* eggs. Once you think about it, do you really think that people will fill their homes with gadgets?

It does seem logical that for some people who have nothing, who suddenly can have anything, there will be a few who go crazy. We will see many interesting reactions to this new economy from the first generation of people who live through the transition. As the global economy works itself into a pattern and people get used to the idea that the global economic network is there to provide us with whatever goods and services we want, those few people who went crazy will look around and wonder what all of that clutter is for. Succeeding generations, who will grow up with the new economy as the accepted reality will not buy wastefully like that.

Other people might buy more than they need to stock up because they are not sure the new economy is going to work out. This is called hoarding. People hoard things when they are afraid and they think there will be shortages in the future. If they trust that what they will need tomorrow will be there when they go to the store tomorrow, they will not hoard things today. As a society we will need to increase production to satisfy many more of everyone's needs. Using more recyclable materials and then recycling products after we use them will be much more important to meet the increased demand. And if we do it right, we will be able to satisfy enough needs so that people will have confidence in the system and they will not panic.

As we will also see later, the transition process from a money economy to a networked economy will be very slow, so that people understand what is happening and trust that everything is going to work just fine. When people understand what is going on and what will come next, they will not panic and hoard things. They will buy what they need and enjoy their lives.

Then, this still won't work because if everyone consumed like some people do, we will use up all of our resources!

It can work. And you are right. We will finally be faced with the problem of providing for every human being on the planet. In the past, the limited supply of money was an easy scapegoat for not creating viable economies in developing nations and for not feeding the world. We could all sit back and say that we would love to help, but we just don't have the money to feed everyone. People did not expect the economy to meet everyone's needs. We expect the money economy to leave a certain percentage of people out of luck and that is exactly what it does.

When we network the economy, however, our producers will be able to take as many resources from the environment as they need to meet public demand. Farmers, miners, fisheries, lumber companies, *etc.* will be able to use all of the resources of nature to sustainably provide for our needs. We will have the capacity, and the expectation, for the economy to use every available resource to meet the needs of the entire global population.

Plus, it is important to remember that relatively few people in the world really want to consume like "some people" do. Some cultures actually find it obscene to consume so much, to fill one's life with so many things, and get so fat. However, even for people who do like to consume, the economy does not have to provide every product that every person wants. People understand that they cannot have everything they want. People will not take to the streets if they do not have the latest version of the latest gadget and they have to make due with the last version of that gadget. The networked economy will have to produce more goods and services than the money economy does now, which it certainly will, and enough goods and services so that people will accept the system. Frankly, if they accept the money system with the terrible job that it does, any improvement will be heartily welcomed.

Food, water and housing will be the most important, must do, and drop dead if we don't things to provide, though, and it is completely possible to accomplish if we would try. We have the capacity to produce enough food and water to feed the world, which is why it is so important to develop water resources. We also have enough materials on this rocky planet to build all the homes we want, so we will be able to build homes for all of those displaced people once we do not have to worry about finding the money to pay the homebuilders.

Outside of the resources of nature, we can also develop recyclable synthetic materials that we can use in manufacturing, which will enable us to manufacture many more products and then recycle the synthetic material to be used in the next generation of products. As we develop more materials that we can reuse over and over again, we can rely less and less on the bounty of nature. In a networked economy, the research industry will also be relieved of a budget constraint, which will lead to many innovations that we have yet to even dream of to produce goods and services for the population.

Governments around the developing world, and the developed world, will also have the economic power to build their infrastructures to make their part of the global network more efficient. They can build better roads, sanitation systems, electric grids, and water processing systems. They can desalinate ocean water if needed to irrigate arid land and provide potable water to their population. They can also improve their education system to better train their population. All of these improvements will increase the productive capacity of the global economy and enable us all to provide for many more people than we are serving today.

The other good news, as I have mentioned, is that 70 percent of our global economy is currently underdeveloped, and could produce many more goods and services. Think of all of those people who are living in squalor and could be using their labor to contribute to the global economy. Think of all of the unexplored and unsurveyed portions of the globe that have untapped resources. For example, the American forces in Afghanistan discovered vast mineral resources in the mountains of Afghanistan worth many times the nation's Gross National Product. The Afghan economy, however, is not properly organized to take the minerals from the ground. We have no idea how much can really be taken from the global environment to provide goods and services to the global economy.

If we can put a person on the moon, however, we can find a way to feed every human being. Once they are free of the budget constraint, the nations of the world will increase food production by every means, including reclaiming desert lands, irrigating every place that food can be grown, and stopping the use of food for automobile fuel.

We can also begin using alternative methods that are too expensive in a money economy. Certain foods can be grown in a vertical growing system being developed that does not need fertile land at all. The food is grown suspended in vertical plastic sheets with rows and columns of pockets where the seeds are planted and nourished with sprayed water and nutrients. Small garden foods like lettuce, broccoli, tomatoes, cabbages, etc. can be grown in this way. This growing method does not require fertile land and actually grows food at a much higher density per square area of land than traditional growing in the earth.

If these foods were no longer planted in the ground, we could allocate farmland for plants that actually require vast tracks of land like grains. In the meantime, these vertical farms could be created in areas that are otherwise useless. Necessity is the mother of invention and this will be a necessity. The power of human innovation will lead us to meet the needs of our friends and neighbors.

Sustainable development will also become absolutely vital to our survival. We have many people on this planet and this new economy will give us the ability to consume this planet dry if we are not careful. Maintaining balancing in the amount of resources that we take from the environment is a more natural challenge than the ones we face in a money economy. In a money economy, professionals face problems like "How can we create a better sales technique so that consumers do not realize that this new type of mortgage product is not a good idea?"

Again, recycling will become much more important. We might reopen mines that are not viable in a money economy but still contain valuable metals. We can mine old garbage dumps and junk yards for metal, rubber and anything else useful. That may seem like a strange idea, but when the economy is free of the budget constraint, it will reach out wherever there are resources to meet the needs of the population.

Here is another strange idea, there is also an asteroid belt out there in space with trillions of tons of heavy metals that could be brought back to earth and used. There is one "Near Earth" asteroid floating not too far away, 20 million miles, called "Asteroid 1986 DA" that is 1.2 miles wide and contains 10,000 tons of gold, 100,000 tons of platinum, 10 billion tons of iron, and a billion tons of nickel.[41] Without the budget constraint of a money economy, our only limit will be our limitless imagination. We will imagine great ways to meet the needs of the whole population.

Wait! I see a real problem. People will fight you because they want their money to make them look like they are better than other people. If anyone can buy anything, then a janitor can buy a mansion. People won't like that.

You know, you are right about that one. In a money economy we measure everything with money including our own self worth and the societal worth of everyone around us. Many people see the drive for more and more money as a test of their own self worth and when they get to a place in life where they have plenty of money, they feel like they have won the game of capitalism. Of course if they won the game, it means that other people have lost the game and the 'winners' can feel good about themselves about their victory. In that sense we do use money to make us feel like we are better than other people.

We also kid ourselves that the lucrative job that makes more money is more valuable to society than the job that makes less money in our economy. That of course is a silly notion. Every job provides an invaluable contribution to the overall economy. For example, imagine if every bank president in the world took this summer off from work. Imagine they all went to some island in the Mediterranean and sipped frosty drinks for a few months this year.

---

[41] "Gems in Space – Undreamed Treasures in a Passing Nugget" *The Seattle Times*, June 8, 1991.

In Europe that happens every August. Practically the whole continent takes off the month of August. If all of the Chief Executive Officers took the summer off, the world would certainly keep spinning. There would be a shortage of mergers or acquisitions for a few months. Things would not fall apart if the vision of corporate growth was put on hold for a few months. Everything would be fine.

Now imagine if all the garbage collectors took the summer off, what would happen? People would have to pile up their garbage in the back yards for the entire hot, stinking summer. Garbage would rot, bugs and rats would come, and there would be more diseases and death in our cities. Eventually there would be a healthcare crisis, and maybe a disease epidemic, all because one group of low prestige people took the summer off. With that in mind, which job is really more valuable to society, the bank president or the garbage collector?

Getting back to the question, though, keep in mind that in a networked economy, every home will be well furnished, so there will be less difference between a mansion and a regular home in a networked economy. In that sense, every home will be very comfortable and perhaps we can all feel like winners. We will all provide a healthy and wealthy lifestyle for our families and ourselves.

We can get over this need to make ourselves feel better with money, though. When we were ruled by monarchies, we used to think that a person with royal blood was more entitled to political rights, like free speech. We got over that. We came to accept that peasants have a right to their opinion, minority religions have a right to practice their faiths, and the press has a right to print the truth even when it is embarrassing to the people in power.

Hopefully we can get over the idea that a person with a lower prestige job has less right to be healthy, to have an education, to eat well, etc. We each have a right to the best that our society has to offer. One of the founding documents of the United States of America, The Declaration of Independence, says that we believe it is self-evident that we all have a right to life, liberty, and the pursuit of happiness. People with less prestigious jobs have a right to pursue their happiness the way they see fit, just like more prestigious people do.

Many people have the dream of making it rich and retiring young. You are asking people to give that up. If everyone has to work, then nobody is retiring early.

That is true. Every person would like to have an endless supply of money so that they can live the life of leisure that they always wanted to live. Just like how democracy got rid of the extremes in political power: the slave and the dictator, however, networked capitalism will get rid of the extremes of economic power: poverty and idle wealth. Once upon a time, when we made the transition to democracy from monarchy, some of us had to give up the option of raising an army, conquering some land and creating our own kingdom where our word is law and our power supreme. Now we will have to give up the dream of idle wealth and unlimited economic power. It will be hard for some of us, but it will be better for all of us in the long run.

It is important to note, however, that since any job will provide consumers and their families a comfortable lifestyle, everyone will have nearly unlimited economic power and the ability to do the work that they truly enjoy. So work will not be as much of a burden in a networked economy as it is for some people in a money economy.

When I got out of the Army, I had a job in a wine store/delicatessen and one of the owners of that little store told me one time, "You know Jonathan, if I didn't have to worry about raising a family and paying the bills, I would just make cabinets. I love working with wood." And indeed, he was very good at working with things but not very good working with people. Unfortunately, he owned a deli, where he had to interact with people all day. But that is another story.

The point is, many of us have more than one talent, and we will be able to live our dreams much easier in a networked economy. While it is true that we will all have to work and contribute to the economy, we will have the economic power to find the job that we truly love, so that working will not be as much of a burden as it is in a money economy.

Speaking of work, why would a person work hard if they aren't making money?

Are you saying that the only reason people work hard is for a paycheck? I think it runs a little deeper than that. People will work hard because they will be doing the job that they enjoy most doing. There is an old saying that if you find a job you love, you will never work another day in your life. When any job will earn us and our families a comfortable lifestyle, we can focus on what is really important, which is doing what inspires us. If we find that job that we truly love, we will not want to lose it, because there might not be openings in a similar job. So we will work hard.

Keep in mind that people will be able to go wherever they want to go, and businesses will be able to hire the best employees and managers that they can find. Businesses will also have the ability to make their working environments as pleasant as possible at no extra cost or burden. If employees all have the power to get up and walk out at any moment, a business had better treat them well. When people find jobs that they love and the business does its best to make the working environment as good as possible, people will be more than willing to work hard and get the job done.

OK, what about overtime? What if a project comes up that requires people to work extra hours? How would they be compensated?

They will work overtime out of loyalty to the company, because they love their work and they do not want to lose that job and risk having to take another job that they like less. OK, stop laughing. There are jobs that people love that much, and places that bring out that level of loyalty. However, if the workplace does not inspire that kind of loyalty, or the work is not the kind of work that anybody really loves, management will just have to give their clients more reasonable projected deadlines, manage production so that sprints in production are not necessary, and perhaps they can hire more people. I suspect, however, that overtime will be a thing of the past when we switch to a networked economy because the employees will not want to work extra hours. Frankly, as we will see, I suspect the opposite will happen. The economy will automate more and more, the work week will become shorter and shorter over time until people spend a few hours working and many hours enjoying their lives.

How will we be rewarded for working exceptionally hard or doing a great job, if employers can't give their workers bonuses?

There are many ways to reward someone for doing an exceptional job. They can be given a public award accompanied by some really high praise by the boss. The old "Employee of the Month" award comes to mind. They can also be given a better parking space, a better office, a longer vacation, a promotion, and/or just a fancier title to name a few ways. Money is an easy crutch for us in several ways. Bonuses are easy and superficial ways to tell somebody they have done a good job. When we move to a networked economy we will have to find other ways to do some things, including rewarding our best employees, and we will find them.

And what about mothers? It used to be that a woman could stay home and raise the kids. These days, things are so expensive that both people have to work and the kids suffer not having a parent around. I think you should make an exception for mothers.

Well, first of all, I am not making the rules and exceptions about anything. I am just throwing the ideas out there. When it comes down to it, local governments will make the laws about the rules for employment and, as we will discuss, the rules for competition between businesses.

But, you are right. Raising and nurturing the next generation is an important job, a valuable contribution to our future. Not just for women, though. There are plenty of men who would enjoy being the person who stays home with the kids. Some writers I know do that very thing right now. That said we should definitely make an exception to the employment requirement for one parent of a school-aged child. If one of the parents wants to stay home and be there for the children, we should enable them to do that. But of course, both parents should be able to work and use daycare to take care of the children if they want to. They should have the flexibility, the economic freedom, to raise their children however they choose.

By the way, we will probably also exclude minors, full time college students, the retired, and the disabled from the employment requirement. Some people are dependents for good reason, obviously, and the economy should support them fully. Students should be able to study or take internships that will help their futures, without worrying about how they are going to eat. Retired folks have already made their contribution to our society and their working days are over. Disabled folks are not able to contribute to the economy and they should be supported as they live out their lives.

You talked before about people buying what they like. That means a person can buy up all the homes they like. There are only so many of those. That means a few people can buy up all of the land and other people won't have any place to live.

You are right. Land is a special commodity, since we cannot make more of it … unless we start shipping people to the moon and the other planets. Once we figure out the demand for land, we might have to set limitations on the amount of residential properties a person can own. Any amount that I wrote would be a guess in the dark. Nations will decide on rules for land ownership for their citizens. Also, I imagine that we will grandfather any limitation to go into effect at sale or inheritance.

Grandfather means that if we transition from a money economy to a networked economy and a limitation is set that a person or married couple can have a maximum of two homes, for example, nobody will have any homes taken away from them at the transition to a networked economy. But, they will not be able to buy or inherit any more homes if they have more homes than the limit allows. So, if a person already owns three properties, they could not buy a fourth property but nobody would take away their property. That way, the real estate limitation will take effect over a generation.

Then I'd buy a whole mess of property right before we switch over.

Right, we may have to nullify any over-the-limit purchases that happened for an appropriate period before the transition unless the person can prove that the purchase was normal and reasonable. Once this idea becomes better known and it looks like we are going to network our economy, any purchases might be subject to nullification after we make the transition to a networked economy. Something like that will probably be how it works.

Those are the issues surrounding employment, unlimited acquisition, and private ownership in a networked economy. None of the solutions that I proposed to these issues are set in stone. My goal here is to explore the many issues surrounding the move to a networked economy, to give the reader and overview. State and local governments around the world will decide on the rules that will apply to their citizens. The basic rule will be that an employed person will earn unlimited access to the economic network for themselves and their dependents. Everything beyond that will vary from one region of the world to the next.

Here is another issue, if I want to go to a concert and I want better seats, I have to pay a higher price for those seats. How can I get those tickets if everyone who wants them can have them?

Let me answer that question with a question: how do we do that today? It is true that the front row seats to the hottest concerts are more expensive, but there are still plenty of people who will pay those higher prices. How do we determine today who among all the people able to pay the higher price gets the better tickets now? What is the rule?

The rule is "First come, first serve" for things that a whole crowd of people want. If we want tickets to the opening of the latest blockbuster movie, we need to camp out in front of the movie theater. For things like the Olympics where literally the whole world wants to go, we will just have to get up early and get our orders in as soon as the tickets become available. We will not have to pay more money in a networked economy, but sometimes we will have to pay more diligence and just get there before anyone else.

What happens when I lose my job! Are they going to throw me out on the street?

No, of course they will not throw you out on the street. The goal for any community, however, is to have as many productive citizens as possible. The more people who work and contribute to the economy, the more goods and services that are available in the market to benefit all of our lives. Also, if people are at work being productive they are not out in the streets getting into trouble. We will need rules that encourage unemployed people to find new jobs as soon as possible, so they are productive.

When a person loses their job, their employer will report the termination to their bank. And when they get a new job, the new employer will send notification to the employee's bank. But what do we do during the period when the consumer is unemployed? In a money economy, the threat of starvation due to the lack of money drives most people to find work, but in a moneyless economy what do we do about unemployment and how do we deal with people who do not want to work?

We can set up employment agencies, using the current network of public employment agencies. These agencies will be networked and every employer who has an open position will list their openings with the public network. That will provide a nice central place for people to look for work in their hometown or across the globe. Local governments will have to decide on their rules for unemployment. After a person becomes unemployed, their local government could give them a period of time to look for a new job, requiring them to be active in the public network of job listings. I am tempted to name a flat time-period, like six months, for example, to look for work.

But then people would work for a month and then "lose" their jobs, and take half a year to find another job. Then they would work for another few weeks, "lose" their job again, and take another long vacation.

Right. So, that will not work. The period of allowed unemployment will have to be short for short periods of employment. Maybe the rule could enable a period of up to six months or half the time they were employed if they worked for less than a year. That way, if they worked four months, they would have only two months to look for a job. Then if they cannot find a job, they will have to take whatever they can find or be cut off from the system. Alternatively, the local government could require them to work in local hospitals, police stations, *etc.* and contribute to the local community. They can continue to look for their dream job while they do a less-than-dreamy job. There has to be a point, though, where if a person will not work, they are just cut off. There has to be some consequences for refusing to contribute to the economy, and we have to use our self-interested nature to drive people to work hard.

The actual rules and time frames that the local government chooses are really arbitrary. Whatever people agree on will work, and the rules will evolve over time as local areas experiment with different sets of rules. We all need to be productive, though, and the rules should encourage that.

Questions About Competition Between Businesses

The government is going to set the rules of competition? Nobody wants some bureaucrat telling them how to run their business!

You are right. That is why the government will not make the rules. This economy will be run by the people for the people. The rules will be set by the businesses that are competing against each other. Nobody knows the market like the people who are competing within that market, so when the new economy is being implemented, each industry will get together and set the rules that it will compete by.

That's even worse! The businesses will make the rules so easy that nobody will ever go out of business. We will have a stagnant economy with no real competition!

That is where we come to the one power that the Competition Measurement Offices will need to have. When networked capitalism is being set up, each type of business will submit its rules to their CMO, which will approve or disapprove the rules the businesses decide on. If their CMO rejects the rules, the businesses will have to come back with new rules.

By what standard will these bureaucrats decide?

The rules should be tough enough so that useless businesses are forced to close but easy enough so that the rules do not benefit just the most popular businesses. A competitive economy needs a market that is tight enough to inspire spirited competition and loose enough so that new competitors can enter the market. After the implementation period, the rules will be set for that type of business in that market. Of course a business will be able to ask the CMO to look at the rules again later if the business thinks the market has changed and the rules are no longer fair or appropriate. So, choosing a market will involve some strategy for a new business, depending on the existing rules of competition and what businesses already exist in that market, both of which will be publicly available.

I still don't understand what these rules will look like. Do you have an example?

Why, yes. Yes I do. Imagine a group of five bookstores which make up the bookstore market of a large town. They will compete based on the number of books sold, which is easy to measure. Here in no particular order is a list of the stores, their average sales per month, and market share based on their raw sales:

Bookstore Market in Town X

Name	Average Book Sales per Month	Market Share (%)
Book Crooks	52	0.29
Sewer Books	988	5.48
Towers O' Paper	8,941	49.62
Book Worm	762	4.23
Great Books	7,278	40.39
Total	18,021	100.00

As we can see, two businesses, “Towers O’ Paper” and “Great Books”, dominate the local market with ninety percent of the market between them. Then two smaller stores, “Sewer Books” and “Book Worm”, do less business, and around four or five percent of the market. Finally, there is a small shop “Book Crooks” that does hardly any business at all. The goal here is to create dynamic competition between these five bookstores.

The simplest option would be to create some minimum number of books that the stores would have to sell to keep their business license. For instance, they might set the number at 250 books per month average over a one year period. This would exclude “Book Crooks”, which looks like it may be some kind of criminal front company anyway. This is a minimum number and it shows that if a store meets this minimum, it has some value to the economy.

But, that’s not competition! That’s just some low bar minimum.

Exactly right. We want the businesses to fight to give customers the best service and the best products. The rules need to set the businesses against each other, so that one’s gain is another’s loss.

And you can’t use the number of books sold, because the market will change from one year to the next. Two hundred fifty books might look like a lot now, but it might not be down the road. You want rules that last.

So the best thing to do is to use market share and …

Wait a minute! Are you going to say that success will be what share of the market you sell to?

That is where I was going, yes.

But if employees are free to a business and if the only measure of success is the share of the market, then I would hire myself as many employees as possible and serve the heck out of my customers. Then I would be the best store.

Right, and that is why…

Then you would have an economy full of fat businesses with a whole bunch of people standing around doing nothing, because they will all hire as many people as possible!

Exactly! It would be competitive but not productive! So, sure, "Towers O' Paper" above sells almost nine thousand books a month, but how many people does it take to sell those books? We want the economy to do as much as possible with as little labor as possible. We want these stores to sell as many books as possible for each hour of labor they get from their employees. And that is the key to having a productive economy without using money.

We can call each hour of labor used a "labor hour" and use that as a unit of productivity. So if a business is open for an hour and ten people are working in the store for that hour, the store used ten labor hours to stay open for that hour. How many books did they sell in that hour using those ten labor hours? That will be their book sales per labor hour and that is how we can measure productivity without money. What is the average sale for the month per labor hour? How ever many books they sold divided by the ten labor hours used, will be their books sold per labor hour for that hour of business.

For this example we will assume that all labor is created equal and we will count an hour that the boss works at the same value as an hour that the newest stock person works. So, now we have to figure out how many labor hours each of those stores used and how many sales they made for each of those labor hours. Are you still with me?

Uh, yeah. I got it. If I owned the store, I would need to sell these books, but with as few employees as possible. So, instead of dollars per hour, I would think of them as sales per hour. I need to hire people who would do the most to increase my sales. If they aren't increasing my sales, they are pulling me back. I need to keep those people to as few as possible; the ones that pull my sales per labor hour back. Sounds like capitalism. I got it.

Good. Here is a new table that includes the number of employees, the total number of employee hours worked, and the average number of books sold in a month for each hour. I assume part-time employees work exactly twenty hours a week and full time employees work exactly 40 hours a week. So each full time person puts in forty hours a week, times fifty two weeks in a year, divided by twelve to find the monthly average labor hours. Part time people work twenty hours a week, times fifty two weeks, and divided by twelve to find the monthly average hours. We can combine these averages to find the total average labor hours that the stores use. Basically, we want to know how many units are sold for each hour that a person works.

Bookstore Market in Town X

Name	Average Book Sales per Month	Employees: Total	Employees: Full Time	Employees: Part Time	Total Labor Hours/ Month	Sales Per Labor Hour	Market Share Per Labor Hour (%)
Book Crooks	52	4	2	2	520	0.1	1
Sewer Books	988	15	4	11	1,646	0.6	9
Towers O' Paper	8,941	35	8	27	3,725	2.4	34
Book Worm	762	6	2	4	693	1.1	16
Great Books	7,278	25	5	20	2,599	2.8	40
Total	18,021					7.0	100

Measuring the market share based on sales per hour worked really shows the value of the business to the economy. Notice that in the earlier table, "Towers O' Paper" had the most market share, but when we add in productivity, we see that "Great Books" is actually the market leader since they have fewer people per sale. Also the two second tier stores looked before like they were about the same value to the economy, but adding in productivity enables "Book Worm" to really leap ahead. "Sewer Books" has a lot more employees. This way of measuring competition is also important because it enables small stores to compete with big stores. A small mom-and-pop store with just them working may not sell a lot of books, but if it is just the two of them, they may have a leading market share because it is very productive.

Am I going to have to know how to calculate all of that?

Not necessarily. The calculation of productive market share is for the eggheads like me who really want to calculate this stuff. Most people will not have to know that any more than they know in a money economy how to calculate the price of an option contract in investments. All you will need to know is that if you have a business, you will need to sell as much product with as little labor as possible. If you do not own a business, all you need to know is that if you have a job, you can buy whatever you need. If you are old enough to retire, you would not even have to know that. Just buy what you need and thanks for everything you have done in the past when you did work.

In addition, because we account for productivity in networked capitalism and make businesses compete only with other similar businesses, this system automatically adjusts for different industries, because while one person could really run a book store, other industries are more labor intensive. If a business requires a certain amount of administration, or a large package handling system for example, all of their competitors will have the same requirements. That is why we compare similar businesses, because each competitor has the same structural requirements as their competitors. So, the businesses will compete not only for selling the most goods and services, but also they will compete over who can prepare, handle, and sell those goods and services in the most efficient way.

I'd get machines to do as much of the work as possible. That way I would need fewer people to do the work.

Exactly. Networked capitalism will also encourage automation. In a money economy, a lot of people think that buying a machine takes a job away from a person, which is less money in the person's pocket, but in a networked economy more machines are a good thing. They free up the employees to do less menial jobs, without taking any food off their tables.

So, how do we develop rules that will set these businesses against each other and provide their customers with the best products and the best service?

We could require a minimum market share relative to the market leader. "Sewer Books" above serves 9 percent of the market demand while "Great Books" serves 40 percent of the market demand. Nine is 22.5 percent of 40. The rule when the network is being set up could be that each business must maintain a market share equal to or greater than 20 percent of the market leader's market share. So, for this market at this time, the minimum required market share is 8 percent (twenty percent of 40). Here is the table again.

Bookstore Market in Town X

Name	Average Book Sales per Month	Employees Total	Employees Full Time	Employees Part Time	Total Labor Hours/ Month	Sales Per Labor Hour	Market Share Per Labor Hour (%)
Book Crooks	52	4	2	2	520	0.1	1
Sewer Books	988	15	4	11	1,646	0.6	9
Towers O' Paper	8,941	35	8	27	3,725	2.4	34
Book Worm	762	6	2	4	693	1.1	16
Great Books	7,278	25	5	20	2,599	2.8	40
Total	18,021					7.0	100

Those market rules will knock out "Book Crooks", who should be having a hard time paying four people with only 52 book sales a month anyway. Maybe they are very rare, expensive books. Maybe the business is a front for criminal activity. If the store is open six days a week, they sell only two books a day. If those rules are accepted, "Book Crooks" will have a year to increase their market share, before they will lose their accreditation. This may seem unfair, but we need a productive economy. We cannot have four people standing around selling two books a day. If the owner of the business likes to trade rare books, perhaps this is more of a hobby than a business, like selling things on EBay.com. They could do this in their spare time while working at another job.

Each increase in sales or decrease in the number of people employed by a store will increase their market share and decrease the market leader's market share. If a business brings down the market share for the leader, it lowers the bar for everyone, since the required market share is a percentage of the market leader. For example, the current minimum market share is 8 percent. If "Towers O' Paper" fired 5 part-time workers, it would increase their market share from 34 percent to 37 percent and knock "Great Books'" market share back to 38 percent, which would lower the minimum required market share to 7.6 percent (twenty percent of 38). Every little bit counts in business. Here is the new picture of their competition:

Revised Bookstore Market in Town X

Name	Average Book Sales per Month	Employees			Total Labor Hours/ Month	Sales Per Labor Hour	Market Share Per Labor Hour (%)
		Total	Full Time	Part Time			
Book Crooks	52	4	2	2	520	0.1	1
Sewer Books	988	15	4	11	1,646	0.6	9
Towers O' Paper	8,941	30	8	22	3,725	2.7	37
Book Worm	762	6	2	4	693	1.1	16
Great Books	7,278	25	5	20	2,599	2.8	38
Total	18,021					7.3	100

If one store innovates and improves its share of the market, other stores will have to innovate as well to keep up. If overall demand for books falls, the businesses will have to scramble to keep up their share of the smaller total demand. Less customer traffic means fewer needed employees, or maybe they will decide to add another business line, like a café in the bookstore, or maybe they will decide to bring in local writers to conduct readings in the store. Since all of the stores will have the same unlimited economic power to buy whatever they need to innovate or advertise, the boundaries of the competition will be the limits of the managers' imaginations. That could get very interesting.

The rule for these businesses in this market is that every book store must maintain a "sales-per-labor-hour" market share of at least 20 percent of the market leader. That rule would stay the same until the rule is changed with their CMO. Over time the market may change, with overall demand increasing or diminishing, the city growing or shrinking, and the population's changing. Occasionally, the rules of competition will need to change to fit the changing reality of the market. So, if a new business petitioned the CMO complaining that the rules were too tight to enable new business a fair chance to break into the market, for example, the CMO might review the rules and ask the competitors to revise the rules.

So what if I am the only book store in town? What will be my rules of competition then?

Another great question: what if you are the only business like yours in town? That can happen in small towns. Or what if you are a new kind of business that nobody has thought of yet? Or what if you are a business with a product that is very hard to measure? A university, for example has a service that is easy to measure, teaching, but many would argue that it's more valuable service is research, which is much harder to measure.

In cases where competition is hard to measure either because it does not exist or because the product of the business is just too hard to convert into numbers, the local Competition Measurement Office can measure a business' required minimum production based on its capacity. A business might be required to function above some minimum capacity for the facilities that it has and the number of people that it employs.

The only bookstore in town, for example, might have to function in line with academic estimates on the maximum number of books it could sell if its employees worked constantly. If a person were constantly ringing up customers, with whatever the average number of books customers purchase at the register, how many books is it humanly possible to rings up, including the time it takes to greet the customer, bag the sale, etc? How much time does it take a stock person to shelve books and what is the maximum number of books that he could stock in a work day? They might add up all of these store functions and determine the maximum capacity of books sold for each labor hour for each employee employed. Then, the CMO may require the business to fulfill a certain percent of that capacity for the number of employees it has, maybe seventy percent, although that sounds a little high.

Universities likewise may be required to maintain a student population that is at least ninety percent of its capacity, and produce research at a pace per researcher that is at least the average for researchers in each academic field. I pulled those numbers out of thin air, of course; the local CMOs will make decisions based on individual circumstances and research for productive capacity across the particular industry that the business belongs to. As we approach implementation, researchers who study industrial systems will develop maximum capacity estimates for each industry and competition measurement offices will use those estimates to create their rules for competition.

You said that the one store could increase its market share by firing a few of its part time workers. That rang a bell for me because people

work part time usually for extra money. In a moneyless economy, will there even be part time workers?

No, there probably would not, actually. I used part time workers to make that example more realistic, but you are right. Part time workers are often otherwise dependent on someone for their livelihood, like students, retired folks, or stay-at-home parents. In a networked economy, there would be no reason for them to work, so they would not. That is getting a little ahead of the discussion, though. I will talk more about that when I talk about how society will be different in a networked economy.

Now that I think of it, without money what will be the motivation for even starting a business? If there is no money, no profit, why will someone start a business? I can't see how someone will go through the hassle of starting a business if they didn't get something out of it.

Not many people start a business just to get rich, even people who start large businesses. And if they do think they will get rich, they soon find out otherwise. People who just want to be rich usually just want the life of leisure that they think comes with being rich, but running a business is not easy. Maybe after decades of hard work, opening more than one location and hiring managers to take over operations, a business owner might find themselves living the good life. That is a long road, though.

Some people start a business because they are the type of person who just cannot work for other people. Others could work for other people but they really want to run their own show. Some inventive people have an amazing idea and they want to see if it will work. That is why I am writing this book. I have an amazing idea that I just cannot keep inside any longer, so I am creating a product to sell to people, telling them about it. Other people just like running businesses, creating a product, feeling the thrill of public approval when people really like their product, and of course beating the pulp out of their competitors. All of those things will still exist in a networked economy; they just will not be expressed as money.

Actually, I believe that in an economy without the risk of poverty for a failed entrepreneur more people will take the leap and open their own businesses. There are many people in this world who would like to own their own business and do what they love to do, but the reality is too daunting. Perhaps they do not understand the financial aspects about how to get the space, the supplies and the financing. Perhaps they do not want to take the risk.

A good friend of mine for example is a wonderful photographer and she loves taking pictures. She could make a great living behind the lens. People whose weddings she has photographed have told her they already had inquiries and they could send her business. But she just does not do it; she does administrative work for a construction company. There is nothing wrong with administrative work, but it is not what she loves. But do not worry; there will be plenty of new businesses in a networked economy.

OK, here's another problem. I got you! I found the flaw. This whole economy is coordinated through the internet, right?

Right.

So what will we do if the electricity fails? You can't use the internet if the electricity goes out. Money works day and night, anywhere, whether the lights are on or not.

Ah! Where will we be when the lights go out? Consumers will need a way to verify their employment when they go into stores during a blackout or in the case of a catastrophe. To tackle this problem we will convert another money-related structure, the paycheck, into a non-money related structure, the employment card.

Instead of the paycheck or paystub that our employers hand us every two weeks, employers will give their employees a paper card each month with the business' federal employer identification number and the employee's information on it, verifying employment. The employee and their dependents will keep these cards in their wallets and purses. If there is a blackout, merchants can take down that information and enable people who have a recently dated card to buy what they need from the store. Then, when the electricity comes back on, the merchant can upload that information to their CMO manually.

Competition measurement offices could distribute receipt forms to merchants with little circles to fill in customer information and item numbers like they use on standardized examinations. During the blackout, the merchant would have customers fill these out listing the customer information and what the customer bought. The merchant would file these forms and mail them to their CMO, where the forms can be run through a computerized reader to download the information and measure their market share.

Actually, once the system is in place, the networked economy could run completely without electricity, assuming everyone kept ledgers. Employers could give their employees a paper card every month to show employment. Merchants could record each transaction with the goods and the consumer's identification number listed on these receipt forms and then in a ledger. Then, weekly, the merchant could send ledger summaries and standardized forms to their competition measurement office via the postal service.

The CMO would add up demand, and calculate market share. The CMO could send out auditors periodically to make sure the summaries match the merchants' ledgers. If a producer fell below his minimum market share, the CMO could notify the producer's wholesalers via regular mail. So, this economy does not actually need the internet to work, but anyone can see the non-internet version is a whole lot of paperwork being shuffled back and forth. The internet enables instantaneous, worldwide coordination. This shows however, that even with an extended loss of electricity, the networked economy could be maintained. This kind of back-up system could be kept in reserve to be used in case of attack or other catastrophe.

Implementation Questions

How long will it take to create this networked economy?

It may take a long time for people in all 194 nations on the planet to learn about this idea and decide to give it a try. Although it could be undertaken by a block of nations who have the resources to create an economic network with everything their populations need. However, once we finally get to the point where we start the transition, it will take at least ten years, but probably closer to twenty years to complete. This is assuming five years to build the infrastructure of the networked economy in the test nation, followed by three years of testing. The first year of tests will inevitably find flaws in the programming and the rules that businesses chose to compete under. The second year will be spent adjusting the flaws in the system and the third year will be another test. By the time the testing is complete in the test nation, the rest of the world will probably have most of their infrastructure in place. Assuming it is, three years of testing would enable us to make the total transition from a money economy to a networked economy in eleven years. If we really got on the ball, we could make December 31, 2024 the day the money economy dies and we create a stable, efficient, competitive economy.

Questions About Living in a Networked Economy

This idea sounds like some silly fantasy of a perfect world. You don't really believe that's possible, do you?

A perfect world? Absolutely not. And this will not be a perfect world. This book is about better managing our economy to make it more stable, productive and efficient, and making our material lives easier. We will not have to worry anymore about making enough money to pay for everything we need today and saving for everything we will need in the future. Networked capitalism will make the economy stable by taking away the limited money commodity and its wild fluctuations. Along with money, we will get rid of the boom and bust business cycle and the recessions and depressions that cause so much suffering. We will also make the economy more productive and efficient by taking away the budget constraint and by using the full resources of the environment to meet the demands of the whole population instead of just the people who have money. We will also be able to use the labor and creativity of people who now live in places with undeveloped money economies. All of our lives will be a lot "richer" in networked economy.

There is more to life than buying things and eating food, however. There is family and love, for example. This economy will not make the more challenging members of our families any easier to deal with, although we will not have money issues to fight over.[42] Convincing our children to study before dinner and to eat their vegetables will not be any easier. Although parents will not have to worry about paying for the constant stream of expenses that come with raising a child like clothes, summer camp, clothes, braces for crooked teeth, clothes, that first car, college, and of course clothes, clothes, and clothes.

---

[42] Financial issues are the number one contributor to relationship tension and divorce. See Rubenstein, 1980; Argyle and Henderson, 1985; Poduska and Allred, 1990; Doyle, 1992b; Klebanow and Lowenkopf, 1994; Singh, 1996; Dalphonse, 2000.

For the unmarried among us, the new economy will not make it any easier to talk to that girl, or get the attention of that guy, although we will be able to spend more time "out and about" looking for that special someone, and we will have the ability to do more interesting things while we are looking for that special someone. In as much as being wealthy and being able to provide a secure home makes a guy more confident in talking to the ladies, though, the networked economy will help with that. Although, she will not need his economic support to make her secure, so he better be nice.

There are also health issues to think about. Creating a networked economy will not automatically find us a cure for cancer, diabetes, AIDS, the swine flu, or any of the other diseases ravaging the human race. Other viruses, bacteria, fungi, and diseases around the world will also continue to evolve, looking for new and better ways to infect us so that they may survive and thrive. The networked economy will help us research ways to fight them, however, since researchers will be able to work on whatever they want to spend their time doing, without the endless search for grant money. The networked economy will also help get rid of the illnesses associated with hunger, since we will have the resources to finally feed every person on the planet.

Networked capitalism will not suddenly make our lives easy and effortless. We will all still have to work and contribute to our economy. This will not be some Garden of Eden where we lay around all day eating grapes and melons. We will still have to exercise to stay healthy. If we eat too much and exercise too little, we will still get fat and give ourselves heart disease, no matter how we organize the economy.

Creating a networked economy will not do anything to help with political issues. Should gay men and lesbian women be able to marry? Should we legalize the possession or use of any drugs that are currently illegal? Should we criminalize aborting a pregnancy? How about burning a flag in protest? Should we use the death penalty for heinous crimes? How much should a government voice support for any one religion? How much religion should there be in our government policies? Is genetic research ethical? How about embryonic stem cell research? Should people suffering through a painful, terminal illness be able to end their own lives? Political issues will continue to drive our vigorous debates in a moneyless economy.

Social issues will also still be around in a moneyless economy. We will still have racism and sexism, and neo-Nazi fascism and all of the other hate-based "–isms" out there. Addictions of all kinds will still haunt some of us. We will still argue over public education. What should we teach our children in the public schools? Should we teach them about evolution? How should our school books address events in our past that we are not proud of, like slavery or the internment of Japanese-American citizens during World War II? Should we teach teenagers about sex and/or family planning? There are always issues of public "decency": How much skin should people be able to show in public? Is there too much sex and violence in movies, video games, and television? There are plenty of social issues for us to argue about.

We will still have crime. Money is a huge motivation for committing crime and a networked economy will get rid of a certain amount of crime; however some people will still lose their tempers and assault other people, sometimes even kill them. Some people will drink too much alcohol and decide to get behind the wheel of a car, causing accidents. Unfortunately, there will still be the physical, sexual, and emotional abuse of children. If I think of a way to get rid of that, I will definitely let you know. We will talk more about how crime will change shortly.

There is no such thing as a utopia. The reason for that is because people are imperfect. No matter how we organize our society, we can never make it perfect, because we are human. However, our goal is not to create a perfect society. Our goal is the same as the goal for the person who first suggested leaving the cave and living in manmade homes instead. It is the same goal as the person who suggested following the herds of wild animals, so we can kill them and eat them all year long. The same as the person who first suggested planting crops and herding animals to give us stable communities so that we did not have to move around all the time. It is the same as the person who suggested building a sewer system to get rid of all of that disease-causing garbage and human waste in the streets. It is the same as the person who suggested that we organize fire departments to protect everyone's homes, instead of one house catching fire and the whole city burning down. Every time a new technology or a new way of organizing our lives comes along, people use it to improve our situation and our communities.

The goal in writing this book is to make a better society and a better world. The Preamble to the United States Constitution lists six reasons why the founders created this great nation: to 1. Form a more perfect union, 2. Establish justice, 3. Insure domestic tranquility, 4. Provide for the common defense, 5. Promote the general welfare, and 6. Secure the blessings of liberty to ourselves and our posterity. That is my goal in writing this book, not only for the United States but for the whole world.

The divisiveness and instability that surrounds using a limited money medium of exchange, and the inequality that comes with it, creates imperfections in our union, undermines justice, disrupts domestic tranquility, increases the number of people we need to defend our nation against, diminishes the general welfare, and makes liberty more tenuous for ourselves and our children's children. A networked economy will make our society and our world more perfect, just, tranquil, secure, prosperous, and free.

What's the down side to a networked economy?

There are actually a few ways that a networked economy will make the world more complicated. The first is that it will make us more dangerous to this planet and make recycling an absolute necessity.

This effect has already been noted, but it bears repeating for emphasis. For those of us who would rather not be bothered to think about where their garbage goes once they toss it out, this is not good news. If we take off the reigns of the budget constraint and enable producers to take as much oil, wood, minerals, fish, and heavy metals from the environment that they can in a 24 hour manufacturing workday, and then just throw all of those materials away after we use them, we would soon be out of raw materials. There are almost seven billion people on this planet, and we are projected to be nine billion people by the year 2050.

If we are going to manage this economy so that everyone gets what they need, we will have to change our philosophy about how we design products. We will need to design them keeping in mind what we will do with them after we are done as I wrote about in more detail above. We will use more recyclable materials so that products can be broken down and their components can be reused. Electronic products will be designed so that new software features can be added in later without buying an entirely new product. All of our products will be designed to be long lasting, and then enable easy disassembly after we are done with them.

A second way that a networked economy will make life more complicated is that it will make participating in our government and keeping it transparent even more important.[43] We will all need to add our voices to public debate and keep an eye on what the government is using its large administrative abilities to do. Why? The government will not have a budget constraint either and it will be able to do whatever it decides to muster the resources to do.

That will be good on the one hand because there will be no more epic budget battles and fighting over whether we should cut or increase funding for education, benefits to the poor, the military, or fixing bridges and building the infrastructure. We will be able to do all of those things. The states and local governments will be able to maintain the infrastructure of roads, highways, bridges, water treatment plants, electric generation and transmission, *etc.* without interference from the federal government.

The federal government, meanwhile, will be able to build an efficient, disciplined, principled federal police force and military, and that is why keeping the federal government transparent will become even more important than it is today. For those of us who like to keep government power to a minimum, keeping an eye on the government will become very important. Unwatched governments have a history of doing some very nasty things in the past, like conducting experiments on unsuspecting citizens without telling them. Either way, we will not be able to afford to leave the government alone to do whatever it wishes. Fortunately, there are networks of watchdog groups who find that kind of work very energizing.

The third way that networked capitalism will make the world more complicated is related to the second way. Networked capitalism is designed to be a global economy. That means that our government will be able to function without budget worries, and so will every other government in the world. That is good for the citizens of developing nations because their economies will be able to develop easier. They will no longer have to stretch anemic budgets to build an economy, or drown in debt, trying to leverage scant funding to build roads and farms to feed their people. It is bad for the citizens of oppressive regimes because those regimes will be able to oppress their citizens easier. It will also be easier for these regimes to provide food and shelter for their people and keep their population satisfied. This will

[43] See Bellah et al., 1992.

complicate things for those people who want to democratize these regimes. People who are well fed do not usually take to the streets.

You listed nine industries that will go out of business, five industries that will fade some, and seven industries that will get bigger in this networked economy of yours?

That is right.

And your networked economy requires everyone to work?

Exactly.

Well, smart guy, will the number of jobs you will gain make up for all of those jobs you just lost?

It is most likely that the exploding demand for manufactured goods and for services of all kinds will far outstrip the available labor even in our vastly underemployed population. The service industry will likely never come to a point where they cannot use more people. This is especially true for the specialty services that are labor intensive, like housecleaning, gardening, or personal chef services for example. Also, the rules of employment that we laid out above create the opportunity for one parent to stay at home to take care of their children. That will lead to many dual income homes to take one person out of the labor market to stay home. Many of those single parents out there will also take advantage of the opportunity to stop working and look after their children.

With all of that in mind, I think that it is far more likely that this will lead to a revolution in the automation of the economy as a whole. We will see technology step in to make up for a shortage of labor in a very busy economic network. The exploding demand and limited labor, combined with the incentive to automate in the way that we will calculate productive market share in a networked economy, will lead almost certainly to far greater automation in our economy.

In many markets today, for example, we see stores experimenting with self-checkout scanners that enable consumers to scan their own goods, pay, make their own change, bag their own items, and hand themselves their receipt for the purchase. They can even wish themselves to have a good day if they like. Meanwhile, there is often one person overseeing eight or nine registers to resolve any problems.

Self-checkout will someday be the normal way a store works and having a person actually bagging a person's groceries will be something reserved for small markets.

However, nobody knows how this might play out. It might be possible that the available job base will shrink enough so that there will not be enough jobs for everyone. If we come to a point where we just do not have enough jobs for everyone, there are a number of things we can do. The local government can expand and shrink its staff rolls to take up the slack in unemployment. They can always use more help in community hospitals and police stations; there are always bridges to fix and infrastructure to upgrade.

My favorite fix to the potential of having a shortage of jobs, however, is to shorten the work day or the work week and spread the work around to more people. Networked capitalism will encourage automation as businesses are driven to do more and more with less and less labor. Why not shorten the work day an hour or two, or make the work week four days instead of five? Why not do both? I vote we get rid of Mondays; I have never liked Mondays. For those Christians among us, it will provide a day after the Sunday holy day. Perhaps other societies with holy days on Saturday will take Friday out of the work week. It is just a thought. This is a good reminder that the rules of a networked economy will be set by the local areas and not by this book.

Networked capitalism will create an incentive to automate the economy as much as possible. Over the course of fifty or one hundred years as the economy automates more and more, we can shorten the work day more and more. We may reach a point where the economy is completely automated and each person will only have to work a few hours a week to keep the economy running. That would be a great long term goal for the economy: to automate as much as possible and require as little human labor as possible, leading to a day when the economy requires very little labor at all.

In any case the labor force will look quite a bit different. Money is a very important part of every aspect of our lives. All of the people whose job it is to manage those various money-centered aspects of our lives will need new jobs. Others for whom money is important but not vital to their jobs will see their industries diminished. And those industries that people would use more if only they had more money will see their industries grow and grow.

Bibliography

Arnold, Thurman, Morris Ernst, Adolf Berle Jr., Lloyd Garrison, and Sir Alfred Zimmern.1971. *The Future of Digital Capitalism*, Freeport, NY: Books for Libraries Press.

Bohamian, Paul. 1955. “The Impact of Money on an African Subsistence Economy”. *The Journal of Economic History* 19(4): 60-70.

Baker, Wayne. 1987. “What is Money? A Social Structural Interpretation,” in *Intercorporate Relations*, ed. Mark Mizruchi and Michael Schwartz. New York: Cambridge University Press. 109-144.

Baker, Wayne, and Jimerson, Jason B. 1992. “The Sociology of Money”. *American Behavioral Scientist* 35(6). July/August: 678-693.

Bauman, Zygmunt. 1998. *Work, Consumerism and the New Poor*. Philadelphia, PA: Open University Press.

Beaglehole, E. 1932. *Property: A Study in Social Psychology*. New York: MacMillan.

Bellah, Robert N. Richard Madsen, William Sullivan, Ann Swidler, Steven Tipton. 1992. *The Good Society*. New York: Vintage Books.

Benne, Robert. 1981. *The Ethics of Digital Capitalism*. Philadelphia: Fortress Press.

Betancourt, Roger R. 1992. *An Analysis of the U.S. Distribution System*. USOECD Department of Economics and Statistics. Working Paper. 92-6.

Blau, Peter. 1986. *Exchange and Power in Social Life*. New Brunswick, CT: Transaction Books.

Bloom William. 1996. *Money, Heart and Mind.* New York: Kodensha International.

Bocock, Robert. 1993. *Consumption*, London: Routledge.

Bretton, Henry. 1980. *The Power of Money*. Albany, NY: State University of New York Press.

Brin, David. 1998. *The Transparent Society*. Reading, Massachusetts: Addison-Wesley.

Brown, L., C. Flavin, H. French. 2000. *State of the World 2010*. New York: W.W. Norton & Company.

Carruthers, Bruce and Ariovich, Laura. 2010. *Money and Credit: A Sociological Approach*. Cambridge: Polity Press.

Coleman, James. 1992. "Crime and Money". *American Behavioral Scientist* 35(6) July/August: 827-836.

Crump, Thomas. 1981. *The Phenomenon of Money*. London: Routledge.

Dahl, Robert A. 1998. *On Democracy.* New Haven, CT: Yale University Press.

Dalphonse, Sherri. 2000. "Love & Money". *Washingtonian.* February 35(5).

Dalton, G. 1971. "Economic Theory and Primitive Society". *American Anthropologist* 63:1-25.

Deflem, Mathieu. 2003 "The Sociology of the Sociology of Money" *Journal of Classical Sociology* 3(1): 67-96.

Dodd, Nigel. 2005. "Reinventing Monies in Europe". *Economy and Society* 34(4): 558-83.

---. 1994. *The Sociology of Money.* New York: Continuum Publishing Co.

Doyle, Kenneth. 1992a. "Money and the Behavioral Sciences". *American Behavioral Scientist* 35(6), July/August: 641-657.

---. 1992b. "Long-Term Health Care, Voluntary Self-Impoverishment, and Family Stress" *American Behavioral Scientist* 35(6). July/August: 803-808.

Dillard, Dudley. 1987. "Money as an Institution of Capitalism". *Journal of Economic Issues*. 21(4)(Dec):1623-1647.

Dittmar, H. 1992. *The Social Psychology of Material Possessions.* Hemel Hempstead: Harvester Wheatsheaf.

Dorn, James A. 1997. *The Future of Money in the Information Age.* Cato Institute.

Drucker, Peter. 1993. *Post-Capitalist Society.* New York: HarperCollins Publishers, Inc.

Easterlin, Richard A. (Ed.) 2002. *Happiness in Economics.* Edward Elgar.

Einzig, P. 1949. *Primitive Money.* Oxford: Pergamon Press.

Ethier, Diane. 1997. *Economic Adjustment in New Democracies.* New York: St. Martin's Press, Inc.

Ferguson, Niall. 2001. *The Cash Nexus: Money and Power in the Modern World*. New York: Basic Books.

Fine, B. and Lapavitsas, C. 2000. "Markets & Money in Social Theory in Social Theory: What Role for Economics?" *Economy and Society* 29(3): 357-82

Finn, Daniel Rush. 1992. "The Meanings of Money: A View from Economics" *American Behavioral Scientist*. 35(6): 658-668.

Friedman, Milton. 1962. *Capitalism and Freedom.* Chicago: University of Chicago Press.

Furnham, Adrian and Michael Argyle. 1998. *The Psychology of Money.* London: Routledge.

---, 1986. *Economic Mind.* New York: St. Martin's Press.

Galbraith, J.K. 1975. *Money.* Boston: Houghton Mifflin Co.

Gambetta, D. 1988. "Can We Trust Trust?" in D. Gambetta (ed.) *Trust.* Oxford: Basil Blackwell: 213-37.

Gansmann, H. "Money—a Symbolically Generalized Medium of Communication?" *Economy and Society.* 17(3): 285-316.

Giddens, Anthony. 1990. *The Consequences of Modernity.* Stanford, CA: Stanford University Press.

Goodhart, C. 1989. *Money, Information and Uncertainty.* London: MacMillan.

Granovetter, M.S. and R. Swedburg (eds.) 1992. *The Sociology of Economic Life*. Boulder, CO: Westview Press.

Habermas, J. 1984. *The Theory of Communicative Action.* vol. I. London: Heinemann.

---. 1987. *The Theory of Communicative Action.* vol. II. Cambridge: Polity.

Hart, Keith. 2000. *Money in an Unequal World: Keith Hart and His Memory Bank.* New York and London: Texere.

Helferrich, Karl. [1927] 1969. *Money.* Louis Infield (Trans.) New York: Augustos M. Kelley.

Hertz, Friederich. 1962. *The Development of the German Public Mind.* London: George Allen & Unwin Ltd.

Hirschman, Albert, O. 1977. *The Passions and the Interests.* Princeton: Princeton University Press.

Howgego, Christopher. 1992. "The Supply and Use of Money in the Roman World 200 BC to 300 AD". *Journal of Roman Studies* 82:1-31.

Ingham, Geoffrey. 2004. *The Nature of Money*. Cambridge: Polity Press.

---. 2001. "Fundamentals of a Theory of Money: Untangling Fine, Lapavitsas and Zelizer". *Economy and Society* 30(3): 304-23.

---. 2000. "Class Inequality and the Social Production of Money" in J. Scott. Ed. *Renewing Class Analysis*. Oxford: Blackwell. 66-86.

---. 1998. "On the Underdevelopment of the 'Sociology of Money'" *Acta Sociologica*, 41: 3-18.

Jevons. W.S. 1875. *Money and the Mechanism of Exchange.* London: Henry S. King.

Kabanoff, B. 1982. "Occupational and Sex Differences in Leisure Needs and Leisure Satisfaction" *Journal of Occupational Behavior.* 3:233-45.

Kellner, D. 1992. "Popular Culture and the Construction of Postmodern Identities," in S. Lash and J. Friedman (eds.) *Modernity and Identity.* Oxford: Basil Blackwell.

Keynes, John Maynard. 1979. *The Collected Writings of John Maynard Keynes.* Donald Moggridge, Ed. Vol. 29. *The General Theory and After, A Supplement*, London: MacMillan, St. Martin's Press.

King, Anthony. 1997. "The Vulnerable American Politician" *British Journal of Political Science.* 27(Jan): 1-22.

Klebanow, S. and E.L. Lowenkopf (eds.) 1994. *Money and Mind.* New York: Plenum Press.

Klineberg, O. 1940. *Social Psychology*. New York: Holt.

Lea, S.E.G., R.M. Tarpy, and P. Webley. 1987. *The Individual and the Economy.* Cambridge: Cambridge University Press.

Le Claire. 1962. "Economic Theory and Economic Anthropology" *American Anthropologist*, 64(Aug-Dec): 1179-1203.

Lewis, Alan. 1995. *The New Economic Mind: The Social Psychology of Economic Behavior.* New York: Harvester Wheatsheaf.

Lindgren, Henry Clay. 1980. *Great Expectations: The Psychology of Money.* Los Altos, CA: W. Kaufman.

Luft, J. 1957. "Monetary Value and the Perceptions of Persons" *Journal of Social Psychology*. 46:245-51.

Madanes, Cloe and Claudio Madanes. 1994. *The Secret Meaning of Money.* Jossey-Bass Publishers.

Mann, M., 1986. "The Autonomous Power of the State." In J.A. Hall (ed.) *States in History*, Oxford: Basil Blackwell:109-36.

Manza, Jeff. 1992. "Postindustrial Capitalism, the State, and the Prospects for Economic Democracy" *Journal of Political and Military Sociology*. 20(2):209-241.

Maslow, A.H. 1954. *Motivation and Personality.* New York: Harper and Row Publishers, Inc.

Maurer, Bill. 2006. "The Anthropology of Money". *Annual Review of Anthropology* 35:15-36.

McKeaganey, Niel and Marina Barnard. 1996. *Sex Work on the Streets.* Bristol, PA: Open University Press.

Melitz, Jacques. 1970. "The Polanyi School of Anthropology on Money: An Economist's View". *American Anthropologist* 72(5):1020-40.

Menger, Karl. 1892. "On the Origin of Money" *Economic Journal.* 2:239-55.

Mitchell, Wesley C. 1927. *Business Cycles. The Problem and Its Setting.* New York: National Bureau of Research.

Parsons, Talcott. 1967. *Sociological Theory and Modern Society.* New York: Free Press.

Parsons, Talcott and Neil Smelser. 1956. *Economy & Society.* New York: Free Press.

Peretz, D. 1971. "Thirty-five Years of Change for the Financial System" *Futures.* 3(4):349-56.

Persky, J. and W. Wiewel. 1998. *When Cities Lose Jobs: The Costs and Benefits of Metropolitan Employment Deconcentration.* Chicago, IL: Great Cities Institute, University of Illinois at Chicago.

Pigou, Arthur C. (Ed.) 1966. *Memorials of Alfred Marshall.* New York: Augustus M. Kelley.

Polanyi, Karl. 1992. "The Economy as Instituted Process" in Granovetter, M.S. and R. Swedberg (eds.) *The Sociology of Economic Life.* Boulder, CO:Westview Press.

---. 1971. *Primitive, Archaic and Modern Economic.* Boston: Beacon.

---. 1957. *Trade and Market in the Early Empires.* Glencoe, IL: Falcon's Wing Press.

Radford, R.A. 1945. "The Economic Organization of a P.O.W. Camp". *Economica.* 12(November):189-201.

Robertson, D.H. 1922. *Money.* New York: Pitman Publishing Corporation.

Rubenstein, C. 1980. "Your Money and Your Life". *Psychology Today.* 12:47-58.

Schudson, M. 1984. *Advertising, the Uneasy Persuasion.* New York: BasicBooks.

Schumpeter, J.A. 1991. *The Economics and Sociology of Capitalism.* R. Swedburg (ed.) Princeton: Princeton University Press.

---. 1956. "Money and the Social Product". *International Economic Papers.* New York: MacMillan. 6:148-211.

---. [1942] 1976. *Capitalism, Socialism and Democracy.* New York: Harper and Row.

Simmel, Georg. 1991. "Money and Modern Culture". *Theory Culture & Society.* 8:17-31.

---. 1971. *On Individuality and Social Forms.* Donald Levine (Ed.) Chicago: University of Chicago Press.

---. [1907] 1990. *The Philosophy of Money.* David Frisby (Ed.) New York: Routledge.

Singh, Supriya. 1996. "The Cultural Distinctiveness of Money". *Sociological Bulletin.* 45(1):55-85.

Smith, Adam. 1776. *An Inquiry into the Nature and Causes of the Wealth of Nations*, Books I-III. London: Penguin Books.

Snelders, HMJJ, Gonul Hussein, Stephen E.G. Lea and Paul Webley. 1992. "The Polymorphous Concept of Money". *Journal of Economic Psychology* 13: 71-92.

Stanley, Thomas and William Danko. 1998. *The Millionaire Next Door*, New York: Pocket Books.

Statistical Abstract of the United States. 1999. 119th Edition. Washington: US Census Bureau.

Veblen, Thorstein. 1904. *The Theory of the Business Enterprise.* New York: Charles Scribner's Sons.

---. [1899] 1994. *The Theory of the Leisure Class.* New York: Penguin Books USA Inc.

Weber, Max. [1946] 1971. "Religious Rejections of the World and their Directions". in *From Max Weber: Essays in Sociology.* Gerth and Mills (Eds.) New York: Oxford University Press.

---. [1956] 1978. *Economy and Society.* Guenther Roth and Claus Wittich (Eds.) vols. 1&2. Berkeley: University of California Press.

---. [1927] 1992. *General Economic History.* Frank Knight (trans.), London: Transaction Publishers.

Wicklund, R.A., and P.M. Gollwitzer. 1982. *Symbolic Self-Completion*, Hilldale, NJ: Erlbaum.

Wiseman, T. 1974. *The Money Motive.* London: Hodder & Stoughton.

Wolfe, Alan. 1989. *Whose Keeper: Social Science and Moral Obligation.* Los Angeles: University of California Press.

Zelizer, Viviana A. 1998a. "How People Talk About Money". *American Behavioral Scientist.* 41(10):1373-1383.

---. 1998b. "How Do We Know Whether a Monetary Transaction is a Gift, an Entitlement, or Compensation?" in Avner Ben-Ner and Louis Putterman (eds.) *Economics, Values and Organization.* Cambridge: Cambridge University Press.

---. 1998c. "The Proliferation of Social Currencies". in Michel Callon (Ed.). *The Law Markets.* New York: Blackwell.

---. 1996. "Payments and Social Ties". *Sociological Forum.* 11(3):481-495.

---. 1994. *The Social Meaning of Money.* New York: BasicBooks.

www.ingramcontent.com/pod-product-compliance
Ingram Content Group UK Ltd.
Pitfield, Milton Keynes, MK11 3LW, UK
UKHW041945190726
13854UKWH00004B/1794